FIRST THINGS FIRST

Roger C. Palms

While this book is designed for the reader's personal enjoyment and profit, it is also intended for group study. A Leader's Guide with Victor Multiuse Transparency Masters is available from your local bookstore or from the publisher.

VICTOR BOOKS a division of SP Publications, Inc.

WHEATON. ILLINOIS 60187

Offices also in
Whitby. Ontario. Canada
Amersham-on-the-Hill. Bucks. England

Recommended Dewey Decimal Classification: 248; 248.6
    Suggested Subject Heading: PRACTICAL CHRISTIAN WALK; STEWARDSHIP

Library of Congress Catalog Card Number: 83-060818
ISBN: 0-88207-290-0

© 1983 by SP Publications, Inc. All rights reserved
Printed in the United States of America

Victor Books
A division of SP Publications, Inc.
Wheaton, Illinois 60187

CONTENTS

PREFACE

Drifting is declaring that life doesn't make sense, that God is not here, or if He is here, that He doesn't care about us. Drifting is an insult to life and the Life-giver.

To have priorities, clear-cut purposes, is the start on a road not just to success (that is relative anyway) but to a life that is fulfilling.

Without priorities, we waste life. It drifts away from us, subject to and governed by any whim or influence that comes along. There has to be order in our lives. Somewhere in our minds there needs to be a listing of what is important, what is first. But the order or listing is only a starting place. It isn't the end. Lists and schedules are not much fun, but they keep us from wandering around, wasting time, or overcommitting ourselves to many things. The order of our priorities gives us parameters, limits. Whatever those limits, we can then develop a philosophy for doing what we do. First things first are points of reference for living.

Life is so short—do you know where you are going with yours? Soon your life on earth will be over, gone. God gave you this life you call your own; you can't afford wasted hours. No matter what you do—whether you are eating, sleeping, playing, or working—you can know that you are living on God's time and in His plan. And you can give yourself over to that. Living with priorities developed under the guidance of God will help you put first things first.

Living with the Rhythm of God

1

We aren't really in control of our lives; God is. We can twist and turn, be blocked and stymied, while we try to make sense of life. It may seem as if everything controls us except God. But we don't have to live that way.

This week I replaced a water storage tank for our well used to water the lawn and garden. When I hooked up the new tank and primed the pump, everything should have worked—but it didn't. I kept running outside to check the flow, then going back to readjust the pressure; and though I did everything I could think of, I couldn't get the pressure up. I decided to replace the pressure gauge. With an accurate reading, I should have been able to get the pressure adjusted. But the pump still didn't work. I spent hours on it and was becoming thoroughly frustrated. My wife said, "I need the water. I'm going to disconnect the hose and put it on our house water system; we'll have to use city water." She moved the hose, came back to where I was working, and said, "I found the problem; there was a kink in the hose!"

That seems so descriptive of my life. I can try to do all the right things but end up wasting hours and becoming frustrated. The problem is usually so simple: there is a kink somewhere. My life gets blocked by little kinks. How can I have a proper flow of my priorities with a minimum of interference? How can I do what I need to do without always seeming to be blocked? How can I avoid the frustration?

What Are Your Priorities?

One evening I saw a demonstration of priorities at the conclusion of a Billy Graham crusade meeting in Boston. As the counselors were busy helping hundreds of people with their personal commitments to Jesus Christ, a lost little boy about three years old was brought to the platform. While announcements of his whereabouts were made over the public-address system, he didn't appear concerned about his situation. In fact he seemed to enjoy watching the crowd.

Then a woman came running through the mass of people. She was oblivious to everyone around her, pushing through people without apology, with no attempt at displaying dignity or poise, running as fast as she could to the steps leading to the platform. There was no doubt that she was the little boy's mother. With tears of joy, she swept him into her arms.

Nothing else matters when you are looking for a child who is lost. That mother's greatest priority was finding her little boy. She ran to get him.

What do you do when you lose your way in life? How desperate are you to have what really matters? That mother knew her priority; do you know yours? Or are you, as she must have been minutes before, wandering around dazed and heartsick. Time moves on; the world will go along with or without you. What are your priorities?

Priorities deal with what is of first importance. Think about your own life. What rules you? What governs your life? Who decides the direction you'll travel? What are the controls? What takes precedence? What is important to you?

In ranking what is important, how do you list your priorities, your dreams, your desires? As you examine your life, is the list of what takes your time and attention different from the list of your personal priorities? Don't be surprised if your priorities go one way but the daily activities of your life seem to go another.

Who cares what you do with your life? Who cares whether you take that new position, whether you go to graduate school? Who cares whether you get involved in neighborhood club work? Does it really matter? Who cares whether you take the extra time to help people or even bother to know them? What difference does it make?

The answer is straightforward: God cares. What you do, to the smallest detail, matters to Him. Jesus said that the hairs of our head are numbered (Matt. 10:30). We are told that before we were made in our mother's womb, God knew us (Ps. 139:13-16).

God knows every detail about you; what you do with your life matters. This second, this hour, today, and tomorrow matter—whether you are taking an afternoon nap, walking along the beach, or struggling with an important company project. What you do matters to God.

What you do matters even before you do it. God is a-ware of your thoughts. As you make your choices, God cares. Priorities matter because they are your priorities and you matter to God. He is guiding always, even when there are interruptions.

There are no surprises with God. When the phone rings, God isn't surprised. When you catch the flu and can't finish what "has to get done," He knows all about it. There are always more demands than time to meet them: more meetings, more informal conversations, more trips, more questions to be answered; there are items to fix, family needs to care for, and people to help. Life isn't lived apart from tension. We have to do all that we do in the midst of all the interruptions, even those caused by everyone else.

By establishing priorities we will have time to do adequately what needs to be done—to eliminate what doesn't need to be done; to know what can be postponed and what can be done by others so that we can live our lives within a family, a community, and a world that has its priorities too.

God Is Organized

There is one certainty—God is organized. He is the Lord of design. He is orderly. God is in control and He is Lord of all that He has created. Though there is confusion and terror and hurt because of Adam's fall and Satan's interruptions, God Himself keeps everything in order.

In the daily morning and evening prayers given in the *Book of Common Prayer*, there is a rhythm to the prayers so that people who use them in their daily worship come to think of all of life as a part of prayer—a constant communion with God. Our living, our moving, our being are all part of the rhythm of our communion with God. A natural link exists between our spirit and the Spirit of God. We enter into daily, continual relationship with Him so that through our whole being we recognize that He is the God of life.

Our first priority is to be God's people—to know Him, follow Him, and live with Him. It should be obvious that our chief priority is our relationship with God. Unfortunately it is not obvious to many people. We need to know that we were made to move in the rhythm of God. Until we do, everything else will control us. Daniel knew that. He warned Belshazzar, "The God in whose hand thy breath is, and whose are all thy ways, hast thou not glorified" (Dan. 5:23).

A Grand Design

To live with God, to have a "vine and branches" attachment, is absolutely critical. If we don't, we will function as those who do not acknowledge God. The best they have is themselves, functioning in a world made by God, but without knowing Him; living by the laws of nature He established, but without knowing the One who established them; trying to fit as a square peg into a round hole and being in fact—always—a misfit.

If we are only material, as some people say we are, then we have no spirit; only matter counts—we are machines. Therefore we are governed by the laws of motion—that's all. We cannot really have priorities. Or, if we are only sociobiological beings, as others teach, then we are what we are because of our genes and environment; we cannot help ourselves. We are programmed at birth to be what we are, just as a computer is programmed.

Our lives are categorized and shelved by various human philosophies. Those philosophies rule people. Some people are victimized by their beliefs; others try to escape, but they are controlled.

Christians can have direction and must have it, for we know that life has a grand design. Best of all, we know the grand Designer.

I talked with a student enrolled at the Massachusetts Institute of Technology about the interest students there were showing in learning about God. He replied, "We're scientists; it's easier for us to believe in God than it is for philosophy students. They try to rationalize everything; we can see God in science and believe."

There is a rhythm to the universe. Nature has its rhythm: Spring follows winter. Bulbs respond to the warming earth. Birds that knew their way south retrace their stepless paths. Mammals in the sea find their special places for birthing and dying. Stars and planets that were "over there" last autumn are "over here" now. They have their patterns too. It is the way of all things.

Solomon, perhaps while sitting in his garden, saw the patterns of sprouting and fruit bearing. Visiting his copper mines near the Gulf of Aqaba, he saw the ever-changing rhythmic seas. Under the night skies he studied the stars and wrote, "To everything there is a season, and a time to every purpose under the heaven; a time to be born, and a time to die; a time to plant, and a time to pluck up that which is planted" (Ecc. 3:1-2).

It is always "the time." This is a time for something in our lives. Every breath that we take and every thought that crosses our minds are a part of God's rhythm in God's time. There is no waiting or becoming; there is no such thing as "later." We are in "our time" now because we are in God's time. Perhaps we are in our springtime, or in the resting time of our winter; perhaps we are in our harvesting time. We have many seasons in our lives, but all of our times belong to God. Our times are in His hands (cf. Ps. 31:15). There is no "better time" for us. We are in our time now. We are a part of the plan of God. Job knew: "Is there not an appointed time to man upon earth? Are not his days also like the days of an hireling?" (Job 7:1)

Burning and Snuffing
Tucked away in Exodus 37:23 is a verse that tells us much about God's interest in us. Moses "made his seven lamps, and his snuffers, and his snuffdishes of pure gold."

H.A. Ironside described this verse as "unspeakably precious":

> No lamp will long burn well without occasional snuffing. Hence, God has made provision even for so apparently

insignificant a matter as this. To the mind of man it might seem of trifling importance as to how a light was snuffed, and what was done with the black snuff afterward. In God's eye, nothing is trivial that concerns the glory of His Son, or the welfare of His people.

The snuffers were made "of pure gold"—that which symbolizes the divine glory, and speaks, too, of perfect righteousness. It may often happen that some saint of God is losing his brightness, and no longer shining for Him as he once did. It is the priest with the golden tongs to whom is entrusted the delicate task of "snuffing." "Brethren, if a man be overtaken in a fault, ye which are spiritual restore such an one in the spirit of meekness, considering thyself, lest thou also be tempted" (Gal. 6:1). Thus will the "snuffing" be accomplished according to God, and the restored brother's light burn all the brighter for it (H.A. Ironside, *Notes on the Book of Proverbs*, Loizeaux Brothers, p. 117).

That's how much God cares. That's how much He is involved with us. He even cares about the rhythm of burning and snuffing.

This rhythm in life includes doing and being: moving forward and stepping back, activity and rest, hard driving and quiet contemplation—it all fits together. You may be surprised that priorities can include "do nothing time" as well as accomplishments that can be measured, weighed, sold, or used. Realizing that, maybe you won't be so hard on yourself. You won't feel guilty when you are lying in a hammock on a quiet Sunday afternoon. You won't be thinking that you should be washing the car. And on Monday evening you won't be wishing that you could be in the hammock, because you've set your priorities and now it's time to wash the car. Everything fits together. Priority living is not slavery, it is a way of exercising great freedom. You can do and you can be. You can live happily in the pattern of both.

Life Has a Reason

We sense our "being," especially in the main events of our lives. Birth is a mystery. What will this child become? How will this new life unfold? Whether a child lives two hours or a hundred years, this is a person who is designed and created and who will be an influence on all who are around. This world will never be the same again because this person has entered it, and someday his or her leaving will make it different too.

There is a rhythm to life. The sages of the past are no longer with us, but we still have their wisdom. They still influence us. Our wisdom is added to theirs, enriching those who will follow us. Every life has a reason. At death we may say, "This is the end," but it isn't; we may say, "He is no more; he is gone," but he isn't. Each of us has touched other lives, interacted with them in uncounted ways, and those persons are multiplied by thousands who in turn interact with thousands more.

I have been with professional leaders who years before were my students when I was in campus ministry. From time to time they have said to me, "One evening we were talking about . . . ," and then they have told me something I had said to them, repeating it word for word as they remembered it. Yet I didn't remember saying it at all. I'd forgotten the event and the conversation, but they hadn't. Those words, long forgotten by me, had become a part of the fabric of their lives. In turn, they have spoken those words to others. So, on it goes.

In much the same way, our grandparents and their parents before them live on influencing us as do all of those who preceded them. God had it all figured out before we were born. We by ourselves could never fit together all the pieces of our lives, but God can.

We Do Not End

There is a pattern, a carefulness, through all of life. When I was a guest lecturer at a theological seminary one time, a professor pulled out a copy of a magazine article that I had written many years before. He said, "Every year I make copies of this and distribute them to my students." The influence of that article goes on and may continue to go on long after I'm gone. If I had died the day after that article was published, that professor still would have been distributing copies of that article to his classes. How many of those students have applied what they learned from that article in their ministries? How many congregations have been influenced by what those young ministers learned? How many young men and women who are considering full-time ministry will have their lives influenced by a minister who was influenced by that article written many years before?

Our influence does not end, ever. We go on, as ripples in a pond, expanding in all directions. Each of us becomes a part of others.

You are where you are, and God knows it. He is there caring about you.

The "ifs" of life can plague us until the day we die; the "might-have-beens" can make us ill. But when we look at ourselves and at God and ask Him for help with our priorities, He gives that help. He has a loving Father's heart. Through God's guidance, we no longer are victims of everything that happens to us. We are in rhythm with the One who made us, redeemed us, and wants the best for us. We are, in fact, free. God wants that freedom for us. "If the Son therefore shall make you free, ye shall be free indeed" (John 8:36). "I am come that they might have life, and that they might have it more abundantly" (John 10:10). " 'For I know the plans I have for you,' declares the Lord, 'plans to prosper you and not to harm you, plans to give you hope and a future. Then you will call upon Me and come and pray to Me, and I will listen to you. You will seek Me and find Me when you seek Me with all your heart. I will be found by you'" (Jer. 29:11-14, NIV).

What are your priorities? You do not merely have to exist! One day does not have to blur into the next, filled with whatever activity or business is pushed upon you by others. You have direction—you have God.

Your Life before God

There comes a time when each of us must prayerfully ask, "Am I open, sensitive to the leading of God, and am I following His leading?"

I need to know His will for me and I want to know that you are seeking His will too, because your priorities, your directions, your goals, are set by God, and I am influenced by you. I want to know that when you influence me, you have definite goals, priorities, and values, so that even the subtle influence of your life on mine will be an influence directed by God. It is just as important to me that you have priorities in your life as it is that I have priorities in mine. The rhythm of our lives must work under the lordship of Him who calls us His own through the redemption of the Lord Jesus Christ.

What are your priorities now? What are your priorities for your church, for your family, for the people you touch in some way? What are your priorities for your nation, for the world?

Each has a particular purpose; therefore, our priorities may vary. How should our priorities fit together? What is important? What is worth working for? What are you living for? In short, what on earth are you doing here?

You and I have to know, for it is my life and your life that I am talking about. It is our lives before God.

I Need Goals. How Can I Set Them?

2

We've all heard the excuse-makers. They proclaim what they think everybody will accept as true:

"I would have been successful if I could have gone to college, but I had to go to work to support myself."

"Those rich kids whose fathers took care of them, they got the good jobs. I didn't get any breaks. Nobody ever gave me anything."

"Some of us are lucky; some of us aren't. I've never been lucky. I've always been a hard-luck person. Nothing ever comes easily for me."

"You have to know the right people; I've never been in the right place at the right time. Maybe someday I'll be standing on the street corner and the right person will come along and my life will take a new direction."

Maybe . . . maybe. Our lives are full of maybes. Still, people point to unusual success stories and they dream. They read about the man who sat next to somebody on a bus, struck up a conversation, and entered into a business that made him a millionaire. Or they hear about someone who was washing dishes in a hamburger place when a Hollywood producer saw her through the window and signed her to a movie contract. There are all kinds of stories like that.

A Familiar Story

I've visited hundreds of inmates in penitentiaries and jails around the country, and I have yet to meet one who thinks he deserves to be there. They are all victims of circumstances. They were in the wrong place at the wrong time; other people have done worse things and gotten away with them; they never had a chance as children; their parents didn't treat them right; society was always down on them; their teachers in school didn't like them.

These are familiar stories. Many of us feel that we are victims too, even though in the next breath we call God "Father."

Though we may not be on skid row or in prison or always feeling sorry for ourselves, many of us are quite sure that something has gone wrong for us, that we are the hapless victims of a cosmic roll of dice.

Psychologists have discovered that there are basically two kinds of people in this world: those who have a point of direction, a control over their lives; and those who don't. There are those who can initiate, act, and get back up again when they are down, because there is within them an inner drive. On the other hand, there are those who are always buffeted by circumstances, believing that some wind may blow good or ill but that they will always be its victims, and that there is nothing they can do about it.

To the Glory of God

What directs you? Is it everything that's happening in society? Is it the economy that's wrong? The government? The mistakes your parents made? The teacher who gave you a poor mark in a seventh-grade class? Or do you have an inner force that makes you a victor instead of a victim?

Look at the people who have had alcoholic parents and yet have worked their way up in spite of sparse opportunities. You will find they are people with inner drive. Look at the persons who have suffered extreme physical handicaps and yet have done more with their lives than many who have had relatively easy lives.

Decision magazine (Aug.-Sept. 1981, p. 7) published the story of a woman dentist who has no arms. When she had completed two years in dental school, she lost her arms in an accident. After that she worked harder than the other students and became a teaching dentist, which she is today. She is driven and sustained by the awareness that she belongs to Christ and that whatever she does, she will "do all to the glory of God" (1 Cor. 10:31).

A person who is committed to the Lord Jesus Christ has an inner drive. "Christ liveth in me," the Apostle Paul taught (see Gal. 2:20)—and Christ does live in me, just as He promised to all who trust Him as Saviour, Lord, and King. He comes into our lives not to make us "successful," as the world measures success, but to make us His, which is the doorway to far more than "success." In Christ, we have a positive sense of identity. Our goals are organized around His direction. We are organized because He is Owner and He is totally organized. We don't even need the verification of other people (though that is always nice to have) because we know God loves us. That is certain. He has so stated and demonstrated, "Behold, what manner of love the Father hath bestowed upon us, that we should be called the sons of God" (1 John 3:1) and "henceforth . . . I have called you friends" (John 15:15).

It is satisfying to be a Christian. A Christian is not a loser; a Christian is a winner. That's not what the self-help people mean when they talk about winners—they have in mind those who worship the dollar, those who measure success by large homes. God's winner is one who is in Christ Jesus, who completely belongs to the living God. Believing and belonging, with a calling, a direction, a purpose, and the security of God's love, the Christian can set his goals and pursue them.

There is nothing unspiritual about setting goals. There is nothing wrong with trusting God and moving forward. Set your personal goals, your immediate family goals, goals for your extended family, church goals, even community and world goals. List those goals; study them. You can begin by dreaming: "What would I do with my life if I could do anything in the world? What will I have to do to get there? What am I willing to sacrifice?"

A doctor said to his nurse, "You should study to be a physician." Her response was, "I'd like to, but by the time I finished I'd be over 40." He replied with a twinkle in his eyes, "How old will you be if you don't do it?"

I know a man who is a self-supporting artist today because he recognized his gift, worked at it, and though he spent more than 20 years doing other work to support his family, eventually reached his goal. He committed his goal to God and worked toward it.

Measurable Goals

Several of your listed goals may seem to have equal value and you won't be able to say, "This is the first and that is second." But by listing them, you will have something to aim at and measure. Goals have to be measurable, something specific that can be checked. A vague, "I want to be a better Christian," is not a measurable goal. A goal such as "I want to memorize the New Testament by the year 2000," is a goal. That can be measured. Don't set a goal such as "I want to be a successful businessman." How will you measure that? Rather, "In 10 years I want to be president of my own company."

Have measurable goals that have specific steps so that five years from now, two years from now, even next week, you can see progress. With clear goals you will have something to aim at, a reason for working. Commit those goals to God. But don't be guilty of what James talked about in Scripture. He warned:

> Go to now, ye that say, "Today or tomorrow we will go into such a city, and continue there a year, and buy and sell, and get gain." Whereas ye know not what shall be on the morrow. For what is your life? It is even a vapor, that appeareth for a little time, and then vanisheth away. For that ye ought to say, "If the Lord will, we shall live, and do this, or that." But now ye rejoice in your boastings: all such rejoicing is evil. Therefore to him that knoweth to do good, and doeth it not, to him it is sin (James 4:13-17).

That's arrogance! That's telling God what we are going to do. We can set realistic goals only as we recognize His lordship over us, over our circumstances, and over our world. Our place is to be with God, to recognize what He wants, to go where He sends, to live by His will. "If God wills" is not a slogan; it is essential to realistic goal-setting. No goal can be accomplished if we work at cross-purposes with God.

Some people, of course, wanting to be so ready for the moves of God, preface everything with "the Lord willing" and call every influence and circumstance that buffets them a divine sign. They think what will be, will be, and they don't plan or strive for anything. We are not to be wishy-washy.

God rewards faithful goal-setting with evidence of His power, but He does it because He is God, not because we are in need of sensations or warm feelings. Do we have to have certain experiences, or are our goals larger than our emotions about those goals?

A Journey

We are not to set goals just to feel good or useful or spiritual, or for an "I am faithful" sensation. If we only seek good feelings, even the experience of "God using me," we will never move toward our goals. We will be the "experiential" victims of whatever happens. Some people call that "moving in the Spirit." But they forget that Satan can counterfeit every one of the gifts and experiences of the Spirit. What he cannot counterfeit is the fruit. That's God's product. Our work is to be disciplined to committed goals. If God gives us warm, glowing experiences, that's a bonus. But we don't live for that; we must move on or we will wait all our lives and we won't move at all.

God calls us to follow because that's what a believer does. We follow Him on His terms, for His sake and the sake of the kingdom. We can pray and trust Him to work, but the answers to prayer are His work. If He chooses to allow us to be a part of what He is doing in the world, we can be pleased. But our goal is not to be successful; it is to love and obey God.

We are on a journey—that's what life is; we don't suddenly reach our goals, transported by some mysterious, unpredictable power. We move steadily forward by the wind of God. As a sailboat with its sails full of wind can be steered, we can be steered too. Our job is to move into the wind, to tack until we get it; then God will use our motion for His plans.

Setting our goals requires spiritual commitment. Having made that commitment, we can and must move forward. God steers the ship that's moving. He makes straight the path if we are walking on it and won't let us fall. He will always do that if the commitment is there. But He does not promise to do that if the commitment isn't there. Make sure of your commitment, then set your goals.

Remember the words of David. Often Psalm 5:8 is misquoted: "Make *my* way straight before *Thy* face." That is arrogance. It is saying, "Lord, I want You to bless the direction I am going; I want You to help me with my plans; I want You to be in everything that I am doing and planning." David didn't pray that way. He said, "Make Thy way straight before my face." That is a statement, a promise to God that as He sets His way, we will follow. "As for God, His way is perfect" (Ps. 18:30). Pray that and get moving. God will steer you. Don't sit around waiting—get going. God knows He can trust you if you have committed yourself to following the path that He makes straight before you.

Define Your Objectives

Achievement doesn't just happen. Goals are a guiding force in what we achieve. Behind every achievement, no matter what it is—whether a college diploma, or Bible memory work, or soul-winning, or becoming president of the company—we need specific goals.

Without set goals we will never clearly define our objectives. They will always be hazy, fuzzy ideas in the back of our minds.

Clearly defined goals are also restraints. Defined goals will keep us from going off in all directions at the same time. Goals set parameters, fences. The piecing together of life's puzzle is much easier when there are edges.

Reaching a goal requires routine, but goals are larger than routine. "Getting there" is not the same as reaching the goal. Routines get interrupted; goals do not. If we get locked into routines, then we are going to be angered by anything that interrupts those routines. Our schedules will become more important than anything else, and we will serve our schedules. Then when our schedules get messed up, we will be messed up too. A planned routine can become an end in itself, and we could be consumed by the mental energy that comes from worrying about coddling our routines. We will burn up our creative forces. Routines change with circumstances; goals are always before us. What is important to us stays with us no matter how many detours are posted along our paths.

With the definition of our goals comes the definition of the steps required to reach those goals. For example, if our goal is to memorize one hundred verses of Scripture in a year, that means memorizing two verses each week, and it means setting specific times to do it. You may need to get up earlier in the morning if that's your best time to memorize, which in turn may mean going to bed earlier, which may mean a total revolution of your social life. In other words, working toward a goal affects every part of your life. Your life is attuned to it. It isn't something you merely "add on" to everything else you do.

Ready for the Unexpected

Goals that are clear and simply defined still need to be flexible. We should set goals and pursue them, but we can't be sure that we won't get sick or have an accident or suffer financial reverses through lay-offs or whatever. Wars may come, a family member could contract an irreversible disease, any number of things can happen. We are in a decaying world.

Some people, realizing this, tend to float with whatever influences the particular moment, refusing long-term goals and concentrating only on short-term pleasures. They figure there is no hope for tomorrow, so they simply live for today. A faithful follower of Christ knows the God of the ages. He is in harmony with God. Therefore he is an initiator; he isn't sidetracked by temporary setbacks or even permanent changes.

God knows about those changes. He knows what is coming for us. We can't see down the road, but He can. He has bigger plans, and we are to keep seeking Him in order to be in line with those plans. The Bible teaches, " 'For I know the thoughts that I think toward you,' saith the Lord, 'thoughts of peace, and not of evil, to give you an expected end. Then shall ye call upon Me, and ye shall go and pray unto Me, and I will hearken unto you'" (Jer. 29:11-12).

Flexibility means not only that we are ready to be turned as God turns us but it means we are ready to receive more than we expect as God opens the windows of heaven. The giving heart of God is far bigger than any of us know—and He is in charge of us and our world. Be ready for the unexpected. Don't be so caught up with what you think you want, or what you think God wants, that God can't do something extra, something more. Someone once said to me, "God reserves the right to give you something better than what you ask for." And that is true. Often God holds something better for us and He allows us to set our goals; though it is an "end" for us, it is only a step for Him. As He helps us toward our goals, He will gradually enlarge our vision to see the next step He has planned for us.

As we work toward our goals, we need to know what we are going to do and what we are not going to do each hour, each day. A list can help show progress. Most people in business know that; they have lists of major goals and short-term goals— that's a big step toward success.

This not only gives a sense of achievement or progress, but it helps us use those wasted five- and ten-minute periods that seem to escape from our days when we have no direction and no priorities. If it is true in business, it is just as true in our spiritual lives; we need to know where we want to be a year from now, six months from now, and work toward it. Then each minute will fit into that goal; we won't waste time.

Once I explained this concept to a group of women who are full-time homemakers. They replied, "Certainly this doesn't apply to us." They were thinking that husbands, babies, Girl Scout meetings, and telephone calls run their lives. But if you are a homemaker, goals are important for you too, because if you don't have your own priorities, your own goals, other people will run your life for you. You will become the chief baker for the clubs and organizations to which your children belong. You will become the primary chauffeur for everybody else's children. Other people will pressure you to do the jobs they don't have time to do. You need to know where you are going, what you are doing, and stick to it.

A Measure Higher

My wife started college when she was 39 years old. Our children were old enough to appreciate what she was doing and would teasingly ask: "Have you done your homework, Mom?" They also knew that they had to help around the house. She had established a goal; that degree was a priority.

Set your goals higher than where you are now—but not too much higher. Some people look at a lower level and are quickly satisfied. Other people aim so high that they are frustrated. Set goals that are a little higher, whether it's a business goal or even a time-use goal. Just as a golfer wants to take off another stroke, see how you can reach your goal faster, sooner, or at less expense. Be glad as you enjoy seeing how God leads and smooths the path for you. Aim at a goal a little higher than you think you are capable of achieving, and go for it.

Having set your goals, get started toward them now! Don't procrastinate, don't wait until tomorrow—go for them now. As a writer, I know the great feeling of accomplishment that comes with finishing an article or a chapter. In fact, the feeling of accomplishment and satisfaction is so great that I have to counteract it by immediately starting a new writing project. Why? Because if I finish something, I will relax in the pleasure of that finished product. Even if it is late at night when I finish, I'll start something new before I quit. No matter how sketchy it is or how little I put down on paper, I have to get it started before bedtime. It spurs me on and gets me started in the morning. I awaken to a sense of challenge. If I have set aside Friday night and Saturday morning for writing, and if a project is completed by Friday night, I will start something else. In that way, I'll not have a tendency to sleep in on Saturday morning. We tend to reward ourselves with sleep. But book manuscripts or any other accomplishments aren't finished that way.

The Value of Simplicity

Simplicity in the setting of your goals will mean simplicity in achieving your goals. When teaching writing classes, I remind young writers that one idea—no more—is enough for an article. The reason is that most of us readers are capable of grasping only one idea at a time. I tell pastors the same thing. If at the top of their sermon notes they will state the one idea they want to get across in that sermon, their preaching will be clearer and easier for the congregation to grasp. If writers and pastors don't limit themselves to one idea, they will tend to keep adding new thoughts and wander far afield.

Even after I convince writers and pastors that they will communicate best with one idea at a time, I find that many still want to say too much about that idea or will want to say it in a fancy way. If I am working with a writing class, I edit to show how tight writing is better writing. Sometimes the students complain that I have cut out a particularly fancy line, but then I ask them, "How does this help the article?" They almost always see the value of simplicity. This is true in writing and preaching, as well as in setting any goals. Each of us needs goals that are clearly defined and achievable. We must keep them lean, stripped down, not fancy. We need to get rid of whatever blocks the achievement of that goal. When we have a sense of progress, we know we are getting somewhere. Even the best archer has to have a clear target. Give yourself a clear target.

Be realistic about your goals. Understand your limitations, your personal weaknesses. Don't plan all your goals in private. Sometimes the best thing you can do to get started toward a goal is to commit yourself to that goal publicly. Tell other people what you are going to do. Declaring yourself will get you started. People whose goal is to lose thirty pounds know the value of a public declaration. As you list your goals and talk about them with others who know you and love you enough to be honest with you, you will find yourself saying, "Why not?" and moving ahead with them. But don't be stubborn about your goals. Be ready to change or adjust as people help you to "think twice" or suggest that your gifts and abilities are not in line with your projected goals.

Yet, and this is the other side, you alone must stand before God with your goals. You must make your own decisions. Most of the things we take for granted today would never have been invented if those who created the items listened to friends who said, "It can't be done." After all the counsel and advice is given, you will know if you should still go ahead. Even then, always be mindful of those early warnings from others and watch for danger signals. Take advantage of the wisdom and perspective of others; they will see things you won't see. Don't avoid or close your eyes to what they say. But having considered all, if you still feel tht your goals are worth pursuing, "commit thy way unto the Lord" (Ps. 37:5), ask Him to stop you if you are wrong, and move ahead.

Goals are not completed in a flash; it is steady progress that brings us eventually to achievement. As we pursue our goals, we will have both immediate satisfactions and hindrances. To use a simple illustration, if I am making a chair I might be set back temporarily by a joint that won't glue tightly. But my ultimate priority is not a tightly set joint, my priority is the completion of the chair. I may rejoice and enjoy the satisfaction of having those joints set tightly and will work until each joint is tight, but I see these smaller parts for what they are—satisfactions or hindrances, not the final goal.

We need short-range goals that can be accomplished quickly. We need to see little goals fulfilled every day, as well as the major ones someday. Only then will we keep moving. Other people or personal problems can't interrupt us for long when we are steadfast in our goals. We will not be crippled if we have firm goals. Our priority under God is to have those firm goals and pursue them.

Not Too Big

Do you have written goals? Have you broken them down into smaller, workable parts? Have you already started on the first part, or are you still looking at the whole? That whole is a mountain, but a few shovelfuls of earth are not too big. Move enough earth and you will move a mountain. Seeing only the mountain will discourage you. It will seem too big a job to start now. You'll wait until you have more time; you will wait until you are older; you will wait until you retire; you will wait until it is too late.

You are never down, destroyed, or bankrupt until you have lost your desire, your enthusiasm, your vision. If that happens, you will want to dig a little hole and crawl into it, and then you will be the loser and the world will have lost too. You aren't finished yet no matter how old you are. Set your goals and get started toward their accomplishment. "Press toward the mark" (Phil. 3:14). As long as God gives you life and breath, go on with Him toward your goals. Make them your priority.

My Values—
Who Sets Them?

3

Who sets your values? What is important? What counts?

One day while visiting the Gerald Ford Museum in Grand Rapids, Michigan, I stood behind two elderly women as I viewed some awards mounted on the wall. One of the women turned to the other and said, "Now this is what Billy Graham should have in his museum. I was very disappointed when I was there; I didn't see any of his awards." Her friend replied, "Well maybe he doesn't have any." And they walked away.

Billy Graham, of course, has numerous awards that could be displayed in the Graham Center in Wheaton, Illinois, but he has not chosen to display them. Is your worth measured by plaques, honors, and awards or by the measure that God uses—your walk with Him in obedience? Each person must face this and decide. Who sets my values? Are they to be transient, founded on what will pass away; or permanent, founded on the One who is not transient, who will never pass away? We often clutter up our Christian values with secular values, measuring what is important in Christian living by what is important to the world. We value large numbers, prestigious titles, important contacts, social position, income earned, collected things. But we can't build a life on those. Whether we live in a cottage or a castle, only what is built on the Rock will ever stand (cf. Matt. 7:24-27).

Jesus Christ "died for all, that they which live should not henceforth live unto themselves, but unto Him which died for them, and rose again" (2 Cor. 5:15). That's the Christian's standard, the measure of God's value. Yet we read, "In the last days perilous times shall come. For men shall be lovers of their own selves, covetous, boasters, proud, blasphemers, disobedient to parents, unthankful, unholy" (2 Tim. 3:1-2). And that is happening. Our values, our system of grading what is important, have been invaded, permeated by those who know nothing of true worth—for they do not know our Christ.

How do you set your values? Do you make decisions for your life based on what you think is "good" for you, or "right" for you? Are you governed by what is "enjoyable" to you? Christians who measure the value of their lives by "what's in it for me" are doing what the prodigal son did. He asked for the portion of his father's wealth that he had coming to him, all that would make him appear important to those who knew nothing of the home and life he left behind (Luke 15:12). And until he hit bottom, he didn't return to his father.

Many people are becoming controlled by their wants instead of their values. Don't let it happen to you. Values are set by the price put on them. Your value is found in 1 Peter 1:18-19. Your measure of value is the value of Jesus Christ. You are "bought with a price" (1 Cor. 6:20).

Our Current Value Vacuum

On Monday, April 19, 1982 I witnessed two events. It was Patriot's Day in Massachusetts, and at 6 A.M. I watched the reenactment of the Battle of Lexington as the Colonials stood against the Red Coats. On that date more than 200 years earlier, Colonials stood for the values which they would not surrender, and many died rather than give in.

Later that day I watched the 85th running of the Boston Marathon near the same places where those early Revolutionary War battles were fought. It would have been a beautiful race except for a mercenary cloud which hung over it. Newspaper and television commentators were predicting that in future years the race might no longer be run on Patriot's Day, but on a Sunday when television coverage could bring in large sums of money. Runners being interviewed were saying that it would no longer be the largest amateur race, but prize money would be offered, moving it from amateur status to professional. The value of the race was being set by the dollar.

I contrasted these two events in my mind. Earlier, I had seen a reenactment of how patriots had fought and died for liberty; now I was hearing about those who wanted to run only for money. Those who served a cause and those who serve the dollar. What a contrast! What are the priorities for your values?

Even the secular person knows that our current value vacuum—where there seems to be no limits to what will buy us—is crippling us, for it leaves us with nothing but ourselves as determiners of what is right. The very reason we need values is that we don't have them around us. We try to be our own measure of what is good, and we can't. We only measure others who are measuring against themselves.

For years people thought they could govern themselves by catering to their wants. Now psychologists and social commentators are admitting publicly what people have admitted privately and to their psychotherapists for years—their own insecurity, anxiety, and the feeling of being adrift.

We who are believers, committed to God's commands, should have known that would happen. Unfortunately, right at the time when unbelievers started looking for more lasting values outside themselves—in short, when the world started looking for what we have had all along—many of us had already begun to absorb the world's values and lifestyles. When drifting people started looking for a beacon light, many of our lights had been switched off.

If we are going to have priorities, they have to be based on something outside ourselves. They cannot be based on our desires, for our desires are always changing. They are tied to us. If I am steered only by my desires and my appetites, then I am like an impulse buyer at a supermarket—grabbing whatever screams for my attention. If I only respond to colorful ads, bright packaging, and urgings within, then all I will have are baubles.

A Higher Absolute

Desires should not set my priorities. I may decide on the basis of my desires that it is a priority for me to have something, or even to be something, but my desires may not measure what I need, and God knows that. Even self-control or self-commitment does not set my priorities; each only sets my wants, for I am still the one setting them. Even a return to "traditional values," which some think of as Christian, is still only a return to man's traditional values.

There has to be a higher absolute—an absolute Absolute. Only people who have, as a higher absolute, a power and purpose outside themselves, will keep going. Their goals, their priorities, will be determined by the One who has called them. Their priorities, and the value of those priorities, will be set by God.

Only those who recognize God as the One who owns them can have true values, for such values are not created from within or absorbed from others; they are given by God who doesn't change. God must give us the priorities we have; God is the One who sets the value in our lives. God is the One to whom we respond. God is responsible for ruling and guiding. Come what may, whether death, financial crisis, illness, or family deterioration, we can maintain our values if God owns us and we take our values from Him and His Word. Personal feelings fluctuate; God's values remain. To know that God leads and to look to Him to do that leading is freeing. As children (Rom. 8:14-16), we follow the values set by our Father, and He guides us in them.

Our first priority is to be what God wants us to be, to function by the values that God gives. God's values will affect every part of our lives.

We think of values as morals and principles—and they are. But more than that, values are a way of looking at life, at other people, and even at ourselves. When I know my personal value, it influences my values. That is, when I know what I'm worth, it influences my entire value system. When I understand God's creating work in my life, I see how He values me. When I understand His saving work, I see how much He paid for me. When I understand God's involvement with me, I understand the value of the gifts He has given to me. And when I understand that, it influences all that I do, whether it is at home, in the church, in the community, or on the job. Because I have discovered Him, I have discovered me. In that discovery true values are set.

A Value That Is Priceless

As your priorities reflect values based on the ethical standards of God and as you are faithful to them, people will trust you. Trust is critical in business, in marriage, and in everyday living. People will confide in you, believe you, work with you, respect you, and respect the Lord who leads you as you live a life that can be trusted. It takes time to build trust like that, but it is the greatest investment you can make. Trust built on God's revealed value system is value that counts. People calculate the future returns of business ventures and are willing to keep working and investing now for dividends that are years away. We need to do the same as we invest time in building trust—it is a value that is priceless.

I once knew a Christian who had a ministry that could have been blessed of God in helping others. Instead he had a destructive life. People discovered as they had more and more contact with him that he couldn't be trusted. He would make pronouncements on values and morality that he himself violated.

If we are trustworthy, we don't need to talk about it. Our lives will communicate where we stand; people will know. We will be sought by those needing someone to trust—people can tell who can be believed and who cannot. The priority of building a consistent life of trust must be of special concern.

Attempt to build trust into all areas of your life. To be a man or woman who can be trusted is one of the greatest reputations anyone can have. Always remember where trust begins: "Blessed is that man that maketh the Lord his trust, and respecteth not the proud, nor such as turn aside to lies" (Ps. 40:4).

Trust is a value, a priority value. Because you trust God, others should be able to say of you, "I can trust him because he trusts God."

The Christian Is Free

Priorities! They are based on values, and values are based on an understanding of God, ourselves, and other people.

We know we are wonderfully made; we know we are gifted; we know we have a purpose, because God has so stated and acted to make it so. Because we know who we are, because we know the value that we have, we have a reason for stretching and growing; we can live with purpose and great satisfaction. That is why leadership often comes to Christians.

Unbelievers may be leaders too, but their drive is only their own drive which is subject to so many things—feelings, pressures, even the vacillations of economics, weather, world affairs. But that is not so with committed Christians. They keep going for as long as God wants them on this earth. They are children of the King. In Christ they are liberated. The weight of sin doesn't keep them down anymore. They have new life; they have a Mediator who is their Saviour and Priest, and the mighty God is their King. That is why a Christian can say, "I can do all things through Christ which strengtheneth me" (Phil. 4:13).

Christians are free to exercise their gifts. They are free to work without being slaves to money. They are free to care, free to love, free to reach out, free to give of themselves without having to "work the angles." But above all, they are able to be disciplined because God is in charge of their lives.

Values and the way we express them are largely dependent on our understanding of God's gifts to us. We are no less valuable or more valuable than others, just different. God has made us. He has given us gifts. We have value because He has put that value in us.

Why has God placed us on this earth? What values has He placed in us? What does He want us to do? How does He want to use us? These are value questions, based on a proper understanding of God's gift giving. Our first priority is to know God and what He is doing in our lives. We can "mount up with wings as eagles"; we can "run and not be weary" (Isa. 40:31)—or we can waste our time and gifts. It depends on our understanding of the value of His gifts to us—and our reverence for them.

The Meaning of Value

I know a pastor, trained in Bible and theology, equipped for pastoral counseling and preaching, who felt that he had to be the one to buy the groceries for the Wednesday night church supper. On Sundays, before the worship service began, he ran around adjusting the thermostats in the building or turning on the lights. He didn't understand his value, so his priorities suffered.

One Sunday an older man in the congregation who did understand the meaning of value took the minister aside and said, "Pastor, go into your study, sit down, and prepare yourself for morning worship. There are dozens of other people in the church who can adjust thermostats and turn on lights."

Silly? Yes, but we all have similar weaknesses. That pastor had ignored his value. No one else was expected to preach the sermon on Sunday morning—he was. Therefore, it was his obligation, based on a proper understanding of priorities, not to do what others could do. He was not being fair to himself, to his congregation, or to God, who had called him to preach.

The day came when that pastor realized that he didn't have to dust the furniture or adjust the cloths on the communion table—others could do these tasks and he could stand in the hallway and visit with people rather than rush past them. He discovered his value; he discovered his priorities; he discovered what comes first.

Mature Christians are like good supervisors. They are multipliers. They pay as much attention to how they help others improve their skills and exercise their gifts as they do to improving their own skills or exercising their own gifts. They are not afraid to pitch in and work hard. They are not above any labor, but they do not neglect their most important job either. They do not forget why they are on this earth.

We used to attend a church where twice a year the basement flooded. Normally, as a Sunday School teacher, I would prepare my thoughts and organize my notes while others arranged the chairs for the class. But on the days when the basement flooded there could be no class. I didn't go off and work on my notes; I got a mop and a bucket and waded in as everybody else did. Together we mopped floors. Priorities tell us when to work on one job and when to work on another. Because we know our gifts, we know our priorities. We will use our gifts best when we see our values most clearly.

A Christian Perspective

If we are going to have a Christian perspective on life, our values have to be centered on the One who owns us. Realize that He determined "before the foundation of the world, that we should be holy and without blame before Him in love, having predestinated us unto the adoption of children by Jesus Christ to Himself, according to the good pleasure of His will, to the praise of the glory of His grace, wherein He hath made us accepted in the beloved" (Eph. 1:4-6).

Recognize that you have been created and established by God for God. Your values are set by God. Don't get caught by the secular idea that your life is designed by yourself for yourself. It isn't. You are part of the great plan of God.

Many Christians do not like to stress predestination, the foreknowledge of God. But we can't ignore the truth that there are no surprises with God. We need to understand that in order to recognize that the actions of our lives, if lived for Christ, are not simply our own doing. God has His hand on our lives. He has known from the beginning what He has wanted to do with our lives; we cannot ignore that. Our priorities, our value systems, give us a biblical perspective on life. This gives a Christian basis for living and fits everything we do—every dimension of our lives.

If we don't allow our values to be established by God, and if they are not based on a biblical approach to life, then we will pick up every attitude and every teaching that comes along. We will be agitated, as James says, "like a wave of the sea driven with the wind and tossed" (James 1:6). We'll be restless, with no pattern, no reason for what we do. We'll be pressured to conform to society's morality.

A Work Under God

Get alone with God and He will guide you in setting your values. You won't find His guidance while rushing around or partying. Get away from the crowd; determine your value priorities. Let God speak through His Word. Ask your pastor for a list of books that will help you clarify or determine the values that God wants for you. Talk to Christian leaders whom you respect.

Setting values is a work under God. Significant Christian values aren't just absorbed in the course of living. They have to be sought. Getting alone with God is not something many people want to do; they can't stand to be quiet. But that's because they haven't recognized who they are as valuable creations or who God is as their Father. They haven't realized what God wants to teach them about themselves. Self-worth is best discovered in relationship to God. Christians know their worth; they are God's children. They need to spend time alone with the heavenly Father learning, "This is who I am; this is how He wants me to live." That's the way values are established.

Our integrity is built on our values. No one can give us integrity—it comes by the slow building of a value system that is followed day by day. Our values run our lives. Integrity comes from faithfulness to those values. The trickster, the user of people, the manipulator don't understand integrity. We won't learn values from them. We will only learn from those who follow the One who is Truth.

If you want integrity in your life, look to your values. If you want values that produce integrity, look to the true One— Jesus Christ—and obey Him.

Ethics: Is There Such a Thing?

4

What priority do you place on ethical Christian behavior? Be careful how you answer. Christian ethics means more than keeping the Ten Commandments. Even unbelievers keep many of those rules.

Most of us would never tell lies or state what we know to be untrue, but do we enlarge on a fact or color our information to make it more "interesting"? A Christian writer once told me that something he wrote didn't really happen, but it was "more interesting than what did happen." I remember a minister telling a story, then afterward saying, "Well, if it didn't happen that way, it could have."

Do we ignore bits of information that do not fit what we're trying to imply or do not make the point that we are wanting to make? Some newspaper reporters and television news broadcasters do that. A great selection process goes on every day in newsrooms; it is called editing. What we read in the newspaper or see on the TV news is not necessarily the news but is rather what some editor has decided is news. He has determined what will be presented as news that day and then selected his material accordingly.

I remember a Christian conference where some 1,500 to 2,000 people were being greatly blessed by what was happening. Then, one person, who appeared to be either on drugs or drunk, was asked to leave because he was being disruptive. The entire press corps that was there followed him out, interviewed him, and made him their story. The public was given no information about the content of the conference, only that someone was asked to leave.

During my days as a campus minister at Michigan State University, students would occasionally hold demonstrations about the Vietnam War or some other issue. One evening after a Christian meeting on campus, I arrived back home and received a telephone call from one of my relatives in Detroit. "Are you safe?" came the question.

"Of course. What's wrong?"

"Well, I was just watching the evening news and saw films of rioting on Michigan State's campus."

"Rioting? I didn't see any rioting; I was on the campus just a few minutes ago."

The next day I discovered what had happened. On this campus of 48,000 resident students, about 50 students had decided to chant protests and parade in front of the ROTC building. But first they called the local television station, and reporters came with cameras. By the time the news reached Detroit, a major riot was said to be in progress at Michigan State University. Some 50 demonstrating students out of 48,000 can hardly be called a riot. But a news editor had decided that it was and made it so on the news that night. We sometimes smile or cringe at the news media's choice of news.

Before he retired, I used to smile at Walter Cronkite's sign-off each evening: "And that's the way it is."

I'd find myself grinning and saying, "No, it isn't, Walter;

that's the way the news editors have decided it is."

A Thin Line

Because we see this happening around us every day, does that mean we can distort truth in our private conversations, making up what we would like our "news" to be? That's unethical. The more we recognize the meaning of being "the light of the world," the more our lives must be governed by fairness and ethical behavior in every situation. Whether or not other people do, Christians are supposed to have ethics.

Do you always express your opinion as though it were fact? Think about it. This is a thin line, but we must be aware of our words: "Everybody cheered the president." (Did they?) "He felt ashamed." (How do you know how he felt, unless he said so?)

Do you misquote people or put words in a person's mouth? Do you get someone to say what you want him to say and then repeat "his words" when it isn't at all what he was really thinking?

To be truly ethical people, we need to know ourselves. We all have within us a selective process, a bias; we are not objective. No one is. We need to know if we are by nature manipulators; we need to know what it is that we like and dislike so that we won't cater only to our own opinions. We may think that we are objective, but we are really subjectively selective.

There are always cynical people around looking for the hole, the flaw, the failure, in something. They keep looking until they find something wrong, and that becomes their complaint; that's all they see. We need to be aware of that tendency in ourselves. Christians can be just as unethical as non-Christians—not because they intend to be but because they select, choose, and fail to communicate exactly what is truth. In short, we also lie.

As Christians, we are to pray about our ethics, search the Word for instruction, and not willfully violate what we know God wants us to do. We are to tell the truth to the best of our ability. We are not to cheat. In our actions and our words we are to think about others.

But all of this is hard to do. We are influenced every waking minute by the world. Christians do fall prey to the ways of society. Some of us have been hurt by Christian businessmen who quote Scripture and steal from us at the same time. We all know believers who bless God and then curse people. Jesus said: "A good man out of the good treasure of the heart bringeth forth good things, and an evil man out of the evil treasure bringeth forth evil things. But I say unto you, that every idle word that men shall speak, they shall give account thereof in the day of judgment. For by thy words thou shalt be justified, and by thy words thou shalt be condemned" (Matt. 12:35-37). And James asked, "Doth a fountain send forth at the same place sweet water and bitter?" (James 3:11) The problem James warned about is still with us. In an editorial in Decision magazine, I wrote:

> As I think about the Pilgrims enjoying that first Thanksgiving in Massachusetts, I'm reminded again that all of us in the United States, unless we are descendants of those who met the first boat, are fairly recent immigrants.
>
> I have been thinking about that, because increasingly of late I am hearing ethnic slurs, racial jokes, and anti-Semitic remarks, and I shudder. I hurt not only because of the words spoken but because I hear professing Christians saying those words. It would be easy to say, "People who speak that way are not really Christians," and maybe they aren't. But they tell me that they are. Some are even in the Christian ministry.
>
> How can that be? I have asked that question and I hear comments such as, "I don't see any bigotry or racial prejudice in that." Or worse, "You don't know 'them' as well as I do."

And I'm reminded of the Christians who said similar things in Europe just before millions of Jewish people were shipped off to Auschwitz, Mauthausen, Bergen-Belsen, and Dachau.

The Apostle James said of the tongue: "With the tongue we praise our Lord and Father, and with it we curse men, who have been made in God's likeness. Out of the same mouth come praise and cursing. My brothers, this should not be. Can both fresh water and salt water flow from the same spring? My brothers, can a fig tree bear olives, or a grapevine bear figs? Neither can a salt spring produce fresh water" (James 3:9-12, NIV).

Will we speak evil of anyone for whom Christ died when we know that "God so loved the world, that He gave His only begotten Son"? (John 3:16)

Three times, in James 4:11, the writer refers to "brethren" and "brothers" to make his emphasis clear that he is speaking to Christians. In short, evil speaking is not only a pagan problem.

James states that the same spring cannot bring out fresh water and brackish water. No matter how we paint the pump, no matter how attractive the pumphouse, the water that comes out is the water that is in the well. You can tell what a person believes by the jokes and slurs that come from his mouth. No matter what he says about obedience to Jesus Christ, you can tell whom he really follows.

It is sin when we speak in a derogatory way about someone. It is sin coming out of the mind and heart. It isn't a word usage problem; it is a corrupt nature problem. Slurs give clear evidence that something is impure inside . . . and Satan is delighted (November 1982, p. 13).

We can tell stories of those who preach loudly about certain sins and then are caught committing the same sins themselves. We know that the "ethics" of the world seep into our lives; we fight against them all the time.

The position we can claim in order to protect ourselves

from the world's ethics is our personal value; we have a high calling in Jesus Christ (see 2 Tim. 1:9). Still, some of us fail to practice what we are in Jesus Christ and the ethics that go with it.

The world's ethics can't control us if we fight against them in the full power of God's might. By focusing on God, we will be sensitive to the One who made us, saved us, sets us free, and moves us into a different perspective of what is ethical and right. We have come "out of darkness into His marvelous light" (1 Peter 2:9). That perspective, that light, sensitizes us to God's scriptural truth and His ethical standards.

Parents teach ethics to their children—both positively and negatively. The lie, "Tell him I'm not home"; the cheating on income tax; the manipulation of others for personal gain—all are lessons clearly taught. Children develop ethical or unethical behavior early.

Time Will Tell

Many people appreciate parochial or Christian schools for their children. They want Christian ethics taught. But in some situations, the ethics are little better in Christian environments than in secular. People who are believers in word are not always so in deed. My wife and I felt that we did the right thing in leaving our children in public schools; only time will tell if we were correct, and that may not be until our children are parents themselves. They grew up seeing evil around them, and we felt a great responsibility for ethical teaching in our home. In some cases the contrast did the teaching for us.

When our children were young, we were in campus ministry. This was during the time of the Vietnam War, drugs, rampant free sex, and all the rest. Our children watched students wrestling with drugs—some winning, some losing. They watched demonstrations. They saw Christians grow stronger in their faith through struggling with the tensions around them, being toughened by the battle. They saw students finding the dead ends of the world and turning by faith to Jesus Christ. They saw all of this and understood much more of raw life than many of their peers.

Consequently, we sensed, as they were growing up and as we talked about life each night during supper, that they could handle what they were facing. We do not always see this ability in those who have been sheltered in more protected environments. Too often we see the opposite, as children are suddenly dropped into a world that they have not experienced before, many to face 18- and 20-year-old temptations when they hadn't yet learned how to handle the 7- and 12-year-old temptations.

Our children always knew the end result of drugs because they had seen how drugs affected others. It's unlikely that anyone will talk them into trying something by such words as, "It's neat." It's unlikely that someone will convince them with, "You don't know what you are missing," because they know things that those boasters don't yet know.

We, as Christians, need to develop an ethical basis for living built on the Word of God. This must be a priority. But just as we need to learn God's ethical standards, we also need to learn how not to be influenced by all that is around us.

Much depends on what is happening inside a person, the guidance that is within. Our children have always known where drugs were available. They have always known where various kinds of evil could be found. In the schools, Christians who have overcome pressure can be a quiet influence for morality and ethics. Recently, I spoke to a Christian involved in the public school system. He agonized over the fact that public schools are criticized for their moral and ethical weaknesses. Preachers are blasting teachers and the evils in textbooks from the pulpit. And there are ample cases to cite.

Yet, as a Christian, this man begged the critical ones to get on the school textbook committees which are open to the public. They have refused to do it. He wants Christians on the school boards to have a voice in teacher appointments. Most can't be bothered. When he went to one of the loudest critics of the school system, he learned that this clergyman not only refused to serve on the school board or the textbook committee, he confessed that he had not even read the textbooks that he was criticizing. He had only heard about them. He was leaving the educational process to unbelievers, then roundly criticizing the system for being run by unbelievers. That's unethical.

The Power That Is Given

When Jesus prayed for His disciples, He said: "I pray not that Thou shouldest take them out of the world, but that Thou shouldest keep them from the evil. They are not of the world, even as I am not of the world. Sanctify them through Thy truth: Thy Word is truth. As Thou hast sent Me into the world, even so have I also sent them into the world (John 17:15-18). Jesus knew what He was doing. He knew the power that is given to believers through the Holy Spirit. And He knew what a difference that would make in society.

Christians have to be prepared ethically as they establish their priorities for life. We live in a twisted, confused world. Navigation of the Christian life is not on a clear ocean, but on choked rivers with shifting sandbars and all kinds of submerged debris.

One does not send sheep out alone among wolves or lambs out into the winter's night, and God doesn't either. He gives us His ethics and His strength. Our job is to be obediently ethical in our behavior and to train our children in Christian ethics from the very beginning of their lives.

We who are Christians with an internal ethical system do

not have to be overwhelmed by all the nonethical people in the world—not because we are avoiding them, but because we know where those influences will take us.

Internal ethics are based on the living Word and the written Word. We can have Christian ethics that are so clear that no one can misunderstand them. Such ethics can be the compass in the priority system that guides our progress in life.

Our ethics are built on God's Word. The Lord speaking to Joshua said, "This book of the law shall not depart out of thy mouth [we are to speak the Word, God's Law]; but thou shalt meditate therein day and night [think about it constantly], that thou mayest observe to do according to all that is written therein [not part of it but all of it], for then [and only then] thou shalt make thy way prosperous, and then thou shalt have good success" (Josh. 1:8).

Remember, the Word promises prosperity on God's terms, not ours; it is success on God's terms, not ours—and certainly not on the world's terms. But we have to meet the conditions of the earlier part of that verse before we can receive the latter promise. First, we have to know the Word, meditate on the Word, speak the Word, and live out the Word; then—and only then—will the rest follow: "Thou shalt have good success." Living a life of Christian ethical priorities means living in obedience to God's Word.

A Revolutionary Choice

I like to read the words of Sören Kierkegaard, Denmark's 19th-century philosopher. True, some called him the "Melancholy Dane," implying that he had many problems; true, he was a loner; and true, there are those who disagree with his theology—but he was a Christian thinker. He knew something of the leap of faith required in the whole area of ethics. He saw that faith brings us to practice ethics, and that ethics influence the priorities of our lives. He saw better than most the differences between the sensual person, the aesthetic person, the so-called ethical person, and the moral person.

A sensual person moves along on the basis of his feelings; what appeals to his senses is the basis for his ethical system. The aesthetic person searches for what is good in a variety of experiences. He draws out from the "sensual cellar" what he believes is good, valuable, right, and true. The aesthetic is a Don Juan, a man of the world, but on his own terms. He decides for himself what is good.

Socrates was an ethical person, having a clear-cut code of ethics that considered others, the state, and the standards of society. But that kind of ethics doesn't necessarily mean living morally because the standards of society may be immoral. The sensual, aesthetic, or even ethical person isn't necessarily a moral person. Our senses betray us, our aesthetics are self-determined, and our ethics are simply that—"our" ethics.

But a moral person makes a revolutionary choice, a leap of faith. He has moved out of the sensual, past the aesthetic, past even the ethical, to a relationship with God. The sensual, aesthetic, or even ethical person thinks of God only subjectively: "what He means to me," "what He says to me," "what He does for me." But the moral person moves into a relationship with the One who is moral. God is moral, just as God is good—that is His nature. He can be nothing else. To have God in us is to have His nature in us. It is incongruous to say, "I love God," while living in any way that is opposite to God's nature. The bridge to a relationship with God is the Lord Jesus Christ. Our ethics are not based on our senses, on our aesthetics, or even on what the world calls "ethics," but on a Person who is morality. He lives in and guides the lives of those willing to have Him as the ethical priority of their lives.

Our ethics are built on a relationship with the One who is above the ethics of fallen mankind. Our best self-ethics is still sin-controlled, still separated from light. We are still in darkness. But that is not so for believers in Christ. If we can say with Paul, "I am crucified with Christ, nevertheless I live; yet not I, but Christ liveth in me" (Gal. 2:20), then ours is an ethic that comes from beyond ourselves. Ours is an ethic given to us by God. We don't boast in it or consider ourselves "better" because of it. We just know where we are and why we are able to live ethically. Christians know that "it is Christ who lives in me."

We may find it difficult to live ethically in a world that at best has only human choices for ethics, but we find that the Holy Spirit living in us is ever ready to help. As a result we live and move and have our being in God. We follow Him; we serve and worship Him. We follow a standard wholly different from anything around us. The only sad part to this is that, unfortunately, many who claim the name of Christ the deliverer haven't always allowed Christ to live in them as Lord and be *their* deliverer. That's why the writer of Hebrews pleaded, "Having therefore brethren, boldness to enter into the holiest by the blood of Jesus, by a new and living way, which He hath consecrated for us, through the veil, that is to say, His flesh; and having an High Priest over the house of God; let us draw near with a true heart in full assurance of faith, having our hearts sprinkled from an evil conscience and our bodies washed with pure water" (Heb. 10:19-22). Baptizing the world's best ethics still does not make them Christian ethics. The world's best is still immoral, for only God is moral. We are brought close to God only by the High Priest; we are washed with pure water.

Life on a Higher Plane
Because we hear so much about permissiveness; because we see around us a paucity of ethical behavior; because people use people; because the sordid, the corrupt, and the perverted are rampant, we tend to believe that Christian ethical

principles and the practice of Christian behavior—which is true morality—are no longer worthwhile. That is not true!

We must never underestimate the influence of a life lived on a higher plane. Persons caught in the social-ethical slough of this world do wish for and even look for another way—for something better. They do watch us. A life built on God's standards, standards set by Scripture and practiced in obedience to Christ, does communicate. We need to know that just because most people live without true ethical positions, it doesn't mean they don't wish for them. They know that their best ethics are still not good enough. They know they need true morality. All honest people—people honest with themselves—know that. Therefore even a few words spoken by a person living an ethical life make people sensitive to the higher way, and they will think about that higher way which they do not have. The void is there; it is in them. We don't have to convince people that it is there; they know it is there because they are made for God, and living without Him will always leave a void—no matter what they try to do to fill it. We may not see immediate changes in the people around us, but we can at least open a window and let people see something better, something more.

I've been with Billy Graham on university campuses throughout the New England region, as well as in other areas of the United States, and at Oxford and Cambridge in England. I've been impressed not only by the quiet responsiveness of many students as the Gospel message is presented, but also by the results months later. Often students who say nothing, who do not respond in any overt way, who slip away to their rooms without speaking to anyone, come around weeks later to talk with Christians and ask questions. In private they have been wrestling with a new way of thinking. They have heard ideas about God and sin and salvation that they have not heard before. (Many Christians don't realize how little of God is known by persons who have had absolutely no exposure to Christianity—not in literature, not in school, not at home—and who don't even know that there is some other way to think and live than the way they have always known.) A window has been opened.

You can open these windows every day of your life if first you will build your life on biblical ethical standards. Such a life does communicate. If your ethics are biblical, every priority of your life will be guided by those ethics, and God will honor your priorities because He will honor you.

But God wants to see that you are truly obeying His ethical standards. Any manipulating, anything sordid, anything unjust or unkind practiced by a person who bears His name reflects on Him. Biblical ethical behavior is an absolute must in the establishment of the right way of life. God is right and just and true, and He will not work out His plan, His priorities, or His blessings in the life of a person who is not ethically trustworthy. Ananias and Sapphira proved that (see Acts 5:1-11).

God, living in obedient, ethical people, will reveal both His ethics and Himself. People will trust us, not only for what we do but for who we are. Be trustworthy, be honest—in everything. Then you will never have to wonder: "Can others trust me? Can God trust me?"

Through prayer, through the counsel of friends, through honest inner searching, examine your life in the light of God's ethical "Rule Book." Then you will live well with the person you know best—yourself. Best of all, in you, God will have a secure, trusted person whom He can bless abundantly. It is His pleasure to do so.

Through Ezekiel, God reminds us all: "I am the Lord your God; walk in My statutes, and keep My judgments, and do them" (Ezek. 20:19). And then He said, "I will kindle a fire in thee. . . . And all flesh shall see that I the Lord have kindled it: it shall not be quenched" (vv. 47-48).

That is still true. A fire kindled by God in the lives of people who will walk in His statutes will not be quenched, and all flesh will see it and be aware of who kindled it. An ethical life does bring results. It is a priority before God that influences every other priority of our lives.

Self-Discipline, a Nice Term—or Can I Be Disciplined?

5

I like dogs—usually. One afternoon in Pattaya, Thailand, I went for a walk with Bill Conard, director, *Continente Nuevo*. Bill and I were working in the pressroom of the Congress on World Evangelization, and we needed to get away for a while to walk and talk.

Climbing a hill, we remembered that we had seen a Buddhist temple in the distance. So we stepped off the main road and started up a trail to the temple. As we rounded a corner, we saw a pack of dogs—probably 20 of them. They saw us, and suddenly the first ones came at us in a pack. They weren't growling, but their heads were down and their teeth were bared. The ones coming in close behind them were growling and barking. We stopped, turned, but realized we'd never get away in time; the dogs were coming too fast. Then a young Thai on a motorcycle came roaring up behind us, swept around in front, and zoomed back and forth in front of the dogs, frightening them as we quickly retreated. Then he was gone, and the dogs didn't follow us.

There is a lot of difference between wild dogs and the soft, domestic, cuddly pets we have in our homes. When Jesus talked about not giving what is holy to dogs, He wasn't referring to house pets. When He spoke of not casting beautiful pearls in front of wild dirty pigs that would trample such treasures underfoot, He was making a specific point: neither marauding dogs nor wild pigs understand the value of treasure (cf. Matt. 7:6).

Jesus was warning us about placing God's truth before people who will neither respect nor honor it for what it is. He was not speaking against witnessing—quite the opposite; He was very clear about the need to go into the world and preach the Gospel. We cannot ignore the Great Commission. But Jesus also gave us the wisdom to know when the precious faith we have will be trampled underfoot and should not be presented for desecration. And if this is true of His Word, the sacred message, the biblical proclamation of Calvary and the Resurrection, then it is also true of the message bearer. We are the temple of God; the Holy Spirit lives within us (1 Cor. 3:16). We are to treat that temple with honor; we are not to desecrate it—not with sin, not with anything that resembles sin. Because we are God's and He owns us—our minds, our bodies, our souls, our time—we must not treat what He owns as having little value. We must not give what is holy to dogs.

Serious About Our Christ

As much as we want to give ourselves to others, as much as we wish we could get into the pit to pull another out, at times we have to stop and say no. The priorities for what we do with what is holy come from God. There is a point beyond which we cannot go in our interaction with those who play fast and loose with the things of God. We can pray for, witness to, love, give ourselves to, indeed readily die for others, but there comes a time when we must say, "I cannot be one with you in that activity." We need to have control over what we do with what God has declared is His temple. We are "a royal priesthood, an holy nation" (1 Peter 2:9). Our priorities cannot be dictated to us by those who don't know Christ. We must not give that right to others. Christ is our Master. We do His bidding. Obedience to Him is our priority.

Satan would love to get us stuck in corners, spinning our wheels over one or two persons who will not repent—letting our drive, our energies, and our gifts be exhausted by the dictates of others who will simply lead us on but who are not serious about our Christ. There are times in seeking the lost when we have to exercise discipline over our compassion and stop short of wading out into society's quicksand. It may break our hearts, but prayerfully, with wisdom and the counsel of others, we must know when our time, our gifts, our self-offering are too precious to dissipate. They are God's, and there are other people, other tasks, and other responsibilities that are part of our obedience to God too. Such a decision requires strong, even at times rigid, spiritual discipline.

On a visit to Fort Bragg, North Carolina, I watched the discipline of the XVIII Airborne Division, a strike force of paratroopers. They are all volunteers. They face the rigors of hard training, the fear of jumping, and the certainty that in any quick strike they will be the first casualties. Because they are among the elite of the military, their training is the best that it can be.

Those soldiers exercise their legs constantly because their legs take heavy punishment in jumps. Once the men are on the ground, their legs must carry them over rough terrain long before any vehicles are sent in. Their legs, so important in an early strike combat zone, will be their only transport. So these soldiers take care of their legs—they run. Every morning at 6:30, 10,000 of them are out running. They run all day long. Then, after hours, even though no one is watching or encouraging them, many of them go out on the roads to run some more.

Why do they do it? Why not do only what they are obliged to do? Because they want their legs to be strong. They depend on their legs. Their legs are going to get them through. Strong leg muscles are a priority.

That's the way it has to be with our spiritual muscles too. We do what we have to do to keep strong, to enable us to keep going no matter what difficult "combat zone" our Christian lives put us in. Our lives require discipline. We have work to do for God.

Our discipline comes from within—only our "within" is more than a need for self-preservation. That is part of it, but also the Holy Spirit is within, guiding us. And He has reasons for making us strong. Discipline is a priority because God's plan for us requires strong spiritual muscles. We do not exercise for show; we do not exercise for others; we exercise because of the impelling of God. Paul could see the need for it: "I keep under my body, and bring it into subjection" (1 Cor. 9:27).

Without discipline we will be guided only by the values or the pressures of what others try to make of us, and that is a wrong dependency. If we give in, we will be ruled—but not by God. We do not present what is holy to the demands of wild dogs.

Slavery at Its Worst

All people are dependent, if not on God then on something else—even on the false notion of personal freedom. Some who try to prove to themselves and to others how free they are have become jokes. They are not free at all. Those who think they are free are often the most enslaved by their profligacy. Their liberty is really ownership, not by the high and Holy One but by the base nature of their own bodies and minds. They are enslaved by the lowest, not the highest, and that is slavery at its worst.

Believers know on whom they depend. They are "slaves" to Christ. If we don't have this inner direction—this slavery to Christ—our morals and our values will be ruled either by Satan's followers or by our own human reaction to Satan's followers; both can be destructive. We have to be careful. Trading our "slavery" to Christ for Satan's "freedom" is a temptation, and even a slight borrowing of Satan's freedom is a trap. Too many Christians are already in that trap—trying to serve both God and mammon. It can't be done: "Ye cannot serve God and mammon" (Matt. 6:24). Discipline means we don't try.

I once knew a man who exemplified the "whose-god-is-their-belly" Scripture (Phil. 3:19). He not only lived to eat, but when he wasn't eating he was talking about food or asking for information about restaurants to visit. Food was his priority. Even his work came second to a good lunch. He was undisciplined. He wanted to be a good disciple of Christ but still eat like a glutton. His real god was his belly.

Watching him reminded me of a little incident I read about that occurred at the beginning of the American Revolution, an incident that may have been a contributing factor to one of the most far-reaching events in world history.

On Wednesday, April 19, 1775 about 9 A.M., the Minutemen of Concord, Massachusetts moved down from Punkatasset Hill and drew near North Bridge. British soldiers who were opposite them on the bridge moved back and sent a messenger to Concord to ask Colonel Smith, the British commander, for reinforcements. Smith ordered out the grenadiers but then made a selfish mistake: he insisted on leading the troops to the bridge. Described as "a very fat, heavy man," Smith slowed his troops. They were not allowed to march past him and he could not move quickly. They arrived at North Bridge too late to help their comrades. As a result, the Minutemen, emboldened by their success at North Bridge, began to harass the British troops. The American Revolutionary War began that day. The Revolution might have been averted that morning, but an undisciplined colonel allowed time for farmers who were still unsure of themselves to become emboldened. And there, on North Bridge, occurred what Longfellow called "the shot heard 'round the world."

The Slavery That Is Liberating
What we are talking about when we speak of discipline in the Christian life is self-control. For committed believers in Jesus Christ, self-control is the gathering up of all that we are and all that we have and even all that we will ever be, and yielding it to the lordship of Him whose name we carry. In Christ there is "self" control, the control of "me" by Christ—the control of "my" possessions, "my" wants, "my" goals, "my" dreams, "my" every relationship.

The "slavery" of self-control is in fact truly liberating because we are under the direction of the Liberator. To the person who does not understand this, such a statement sounds like a contradiction. How can one be free and yet be "owned" and "controlled"? But it is not a contradiction at all. It is rather an awareness of who made us, redeemed us, and now calls us His own and lives in us. "True liberty" is being owned by the One who understands true liberty because He *is* true liberty. Jesus said, "If the Son therefore shall make you free, ye shall be free indeed" (John 8:36). Only those who have made such a commitment to this true liberty can truly practice discipline. They alone live and function within the framework of the very One who created all things and in whom all things hold together.

Discipline keeps us from living empty, dissipated lives. As disciplined people we are not wandering aimlessly without purpose; we are not wondering all the time where we are or where we are going. We know that God knows where we are and where we are going, and in that freedom and peace we move out and really live.

How does discipline work? Chrysler Corporation President Lee Iacocca teaches six disciplines for setting priorities:

1. Make the best of the worst that can happen to you. [When Iacocca was 15 years old, he was bedridden for 6 months with rheumatic fever. He couldn't be physical so he was cerebral—reading everything that he could. That reading background gave him the broad education that helped him in college and in his career.]

2. Maintain the highest possible value system and always work to make it a success, so it can make you a success.

3. When faced with a hang-tough problem, figure out what is causing the problem and then give your highest priority to overcoming that "cause." [In other words, take the problem apart and fix the broken part, just as mechanics fix a broken part. Then the whole system works.]

4. In hanging tough, never be afraid to do the unconventional.

5. Get others involved in your problems. In most cases, you simply cannot do everything alone.

6. Build your own dreams. Don't just solve problems—reach for a dream (William Barry Furlong, "Chrysler's Lee Iacocca," *The Saturday Evening Post*, March 1982, pp. 72ff).

The Road to Accomplishment

Plan your life and live that plan. Plan it before God. Remember the warning in James 4 about arrogance, then claim Psalm 37:5—commit, trust, and God will bring it to pass.

Just as every good business has a plan and works it, we have to know where we want to be 5 years from now, 10 years from now, 20—and work toward it. What will it take to get there? Do your gifts, your skills, fit in with what it is going to take to get there? Be realistic. Plan on the basis of what you are— your talents, your gifts; then, disciplined by the control of God, you can start along the road to accomplishment.

Will you ever be blocked? Yes, from time to time you will. Somebody once asked a group of salesmen what they do when they are dry or blocked, because if they are not selling they are not going to eat regularly. What disciplines get them going and keep them going? Their suggestions are worth noting.

First, be sure that the problem is not medical; you can fight against illness for a while but not for long. Better to treat it early.

Second, be positive. Overconcentration on the negative aspects of what you are doing can drain your energy and then you can't do your best work. Many salesmen give themselves a tougher schedule when they are depressed or tired so that they can shake the negative condition that influences them with the positive pressure of work.

Third, look for little challenges in your daily routine. If your schedule is overly heavy, concentrate on one part of it at a time and do that one part well so that you are not overwhelmed by the big picture. If there are many fragmented, little things to do, get the routine jobs out of the way first so that the major projects are all that you have left to think about. Then your energies won't be drained off by all those little things dragging on your mind. Do the unpleasant things first. Use your brightest hours as your most creative times. Don't use your "good hours" doing time-consuming busywork, things that you can do later with a blurry mind.

You have to know yourself and discipline your time or you will tend to waste time doing the lesser jobs and never get to the major ones. Bogged down with details, you will never accomplish your priorities or fulfill your goals. You will waste hours, days, months, until you find that you have wasted your life.

Don't give up. There will always be setbacks in your progress. This is to be expected. Nothing goes along according to schedule all the time. That's not necessarily bad, because while you are waiting and perhaps churning inside and feeling as if you are spinning your wheels, God in His wisdom is moving your life along in a new way that is going to make the end result better for you. You may think you have been sidetracked, but God is the One who controls the seasons, the rain, and the sun. Always be aware of who owns you as you work out your plan.

We are not a waiting people by nature; we have to learn to wait. We need to know when to hurry ahead and when to be content with waiting, knowing that the road will open up. When it opens, we will be ready to go down that road. We are used to instant soup, instant coffee, and computers that kick out results right away. But life isn't instant. Sometimes long periods go by with no measurable results. We need to discipline ourselves for those long periods, believing that our goals will be met someday in some way. There is great joy in waiting for God to act because for Him it isn't wasted time. God works, even as we sleep. "How precious it is, Lord, to realize that You are thinking about me constantly! I can't even count how many times a day Your thoughts turn toward me. And when I waken in the morning, You are still thinking of me!" (Ps. 139:17-18, TLB).

Holding On
Discipline says we start where we are and keep moving, clinging tightly to God, knowing that there will be times when the waves will wash over us and other times when those waves will carry us out beyond the rocks to the great open sea. At times we won't be making progress. We will just be holding on to keep from being swept overboard and drowned.

Scripture talks about being steadfast and unmovable (1 Cor. 15:58). Scripture also talks about being tossed about like the waves of the sea (James 1:6). Steady discipline, holding on, is not a common trait for most of us; it is one that we have to develop.

Office waiting rooms are wonderful places if you don't let the waiting get you down. You know how it goes when you visit the doctor's office. You sit in the waiting room, having arrived 15 minutes early for your 2 o'clock appointment, and you are still there at 2:30, then 2:45. By then you are churning inside and your blood pressure, which is the first thing the nurse will check, is soaring. At 2:50 the nurse takes you into another room, checks your blood pressure, tells you to take off most of your clothes and says, "The doctor will be right in." Thirty minutes later, the doctor arrives. You've paced the floor, memorized the wording of the diplomas on the wall, counted the swirls on the ceiling tile, and wondered if they have forgotten you and gone home for the day.

Waiting doesn't bother me anymore. I've found that waiting is a rewarding time because now I control it. I always have books to read, and I save an interesting one for what I know will be a waiting time. I start it in the waiting room, take it with me into the examining room, and continue to read it there, no longer fretting when the doctor is late because he has given me an opportunity for more reading.

Most of us try to be disciplined. We set our schedules, arrange our calendars, make our appointments, arrive early to keep them, and then are kept waiting. You can either use the time or let that time ruin you. Some people spend all their time fretting. I used to do that too and sometimes I still do, but I'm learning. I know that a plane can't take off on time if it hasn't even arrived at the gate. I may be able to check other flights, but beyond that I have to wait. I can't control fog, snow, or mechanical failures. Discipline means being ready for the unexpected so that nothing blocks the pursuit of an ongoing priority. We don't have to be victims. Those who let themselves be controlled by events around them, who have no discipline, don't keep going. They are overwhelmed by something called "circumstances."

Forces We Can't Control

Does that mean that God is impotent and that we have to be ready for what seems like His failures? Not at all. It means we are ready to stand or walk or run, whatever is required. The ongoing priorities in our lives, governed by our disciplined pursuit of them, are not blocked by the forces we can't control.

God can even make airplanes fly. He doesn't have to and doesn't always, but I've seen Him do it. One time God moved an airplane for me. Maybe it was to prove to me that He is able to do anything. I was prepared to wait, but God kept me moving. It is an example of what He can do in all of life.

During a series of Billy Graham crusades in India, an event occurred that called for an immediate change in the next issue of Decision magazine. I had the story and I had the photos. But the magazine was in Minneapolis already on its way to the printer, and I was in Madras—halfway around the world. I could telex the story, but the photos were in my hands and the layout couldn't be completed without them. I needed to get from Madras to Minneapolis by the next day.

I left Madras in the late evening and a few hours later was on a flight out of New Delhi, knowing that I had to make one more stop before arriving in Frankfurt, where the connection to Chicago was tight. As we approached Teheran, Iran, which was to be the next stop (this was before the exile of the Shah of Iran and the hostage crisis), I heard that we were scheduled for an hour and a half on the ground, which would mean missing my connection in Frankfurt. I prayed, "Lord, You know the situation. If You want this job done, You can get me where I have to be. If You don't, I'm content to wait and see what other answer You have." As we came into Teheran, the pilot announced, "Ladies and gentlemen, the airport is going to be closed shortly for military maneuvers. We have only a few minutes to take on fuel; therefore, we ask that you all stay on the plane." I sat back and breathed, "Thank You, Lord." In 20 minutes we were off the ground again, the last plane out before the airport closed. I got to Frankfurt, ran for my gate and, with five minutes to spare, boarded my plane for Chicago. From Chicaago it is only an hour to Minneapolis, and we made the changes in the magazine. I felt as if even the military of Iran was controlled (without their knowing it) by the hand of God.

When we find these gifts being given to us, we thank Him. If we don't have these gifts, we thank Him too because He knows our needs and what we have to do. As Paul could rejoice and be content whether he was abased or abounding (see Phil. 4:11-13), so can we. God can and does smooth the road for us—sometimes. Other times He doesn't. The reasons are known to Him.

Discipline is even more important on days when nothing seems to be falling into place. We don't know why we have unproductive days, but God does. Some say our productivity has something to do with the ions in the wind affecting our body. Some say we are influenced by the phases of the moon. Others point to our body's sleep cycle. Whatever it is, we have "good days" and "bad days." Expect it. Accept the "bad" as part of life; don't let it overwhelm you. Instead, work with it. Discipline tells you that you can go on because God controls even your sleep cycles. There isn't a thing about us He doesn't know. He directs all things; we are not victims.

You will learn most about discipline through adversity. Anyone can survive the good times. But in adversity, will you stop pursuing your goals? Will difficulties influence your attitude or will you practice faithful, obedient discipline?

You need a routine, steps to implement when the dry

seasons come. You need to know ahead of time what you are going to do when the blocks come, when the depression comes, when the low points come. You can redeem the time, always keeping before you the awareness that you are God's and are still on the right track. This is all part of discipline. Knowing what we are going to do, even on the days when we don't feel like it, is a mark of maturity. Discipline is the essential ingredient to pressing on. It is basic to the exercise of faith.

We are surrounded by a great "cloud of witnesses" (Heb. 12:1), whose lives were governed by the discipline of faithfulness, and the result is listed in Scripture for all to read: "God is not ashamed to be called their God; for He hath prepared for them a city" (Heb. 11:16).

As men and women of faith with a heritage of disciplined people behind us and a city prepared before us, we press on. For us, discipline is not simply a nice word; it is the basis of our faithfulness. It is a priority for living.

You Can Be Consistent Every Day

6

We do not live in sterile isolation; we are not separate from all of the pulling, wrenching, and pushing of life. Most of us, in a moment of exasperation, have exclaimed: "It might be easy to be consistent in values, goals, ethics, and the whole pursuit of my priorities somewhere else—but I live here!"

In my years of traveling with the Billy Graham Team, I've been impressed by the consistency of their courtesy. Whether they are relating to a waitress in a coffee shop, an airline ticket agent, or an usher at a Crusade meeting, they always give a word of greeting, or say thank you. They do something that says, "You are special."

Others notice it too, and as I interview people for the articles that I write, invariably one of the comments that comes is about the warmth, the courtesy, the helpfulness of Team people. And it is contagious. Just being around people like that makes me want to be more courteous too. I start to see people not as individuals who are supposed to "do" something to help me but as persons who are valuable in their own right.

Courtesy, whether it is a kind word, a helpful act, or a pleasant smile, costs so little. The person appreciated feels better, and the one doing the appreciating feels better too.

The practice of courtesy in little ways every day will brighten a day, raise the value-consciousness of people, and make others want to be courteous too. The opposite is just as true. A sullen, abusive "user" soon has everyone around him angry and upset. A Christian must work at consistency. It is not a fair-weather, good-time virtue; it is a vital part of life played out every day.

As the "light of the world," the "salt," the "city on a hill," no Christian should want to be anything but consistent. There is no other way to live—not in Christ there isn't.

Does what you practice square with what you preach and teach? Is it a priority of your life to be a consistent, faithful follower of Christ, whether or not anyone is watching?

We have all met people who are one way in public and another way in private. There is the man who praises his boss' ideas when the boss is in the room but criticizes him later at a party. There is the woman who claims to love her husband but talks about him in negative ways to other women. There is the person who really thinks he is broadminded because he tries to be that way in some situations but who is narrow, even bigoted, in other situations.

None of us is immune to duplicity, yet we would like to overcome it. If our priority is to grow "in the nurture and admonition of the Lord" (Eph. 6:4), how can we do it? If we want to be more like Christ, if we want it to be true that whatever we do in word or deed, we do all to the glory of God (Col. 3:17), why doesn't it happen easily?

Satan Has a Good Memory

We are all in a struggle, a growth process, a time of becoming; it is painful to see how far short we come even after years of growth. Just when we think we have overcome an inconsistency, it shows up again. Satan has a good memory; he always has new ways to trip us with our old sins.

One Sunday morning I taught an adult class on the control of the tongue as taught in James 3. It was a good lesson and I felt good about it. People told me that they had learned some key points, which is always pleasing to a teacher. I went home glowing.

The next morning, during my devotions, I stopped talking to God and blew up at one of the children, the explosive outpouring of an anger that had been building up inside me for several days.

Tiptoeing around me, the family let out a relieved, collective sigh when I left the house for the office. But that wasn't the end of it. By midday I had exploded again, this time to a person who tends to be lazy; he won't do his own work. So fewer than 24 hours after teaching a biblical message on the tongue, I had twice done the very thing James warned about. Deep down inside I was sick about it. Whatever pain I caused others was at least matched by the pain I had brought upon myself.

I know one thing for certain; a person can learn the Bible, teach the Bible, and talk about obeying the Bible, but still not have it take root in his life. What really counts, as James taught, is what is inside.

We can absorb all there is about biblical principles, and establish Scripture-based priorities, but until they are personal, and consistently put into practice in our lives, until they are a part of our very being and living, we haven't learned.

"I've said it once and I'll say it again and again: I will obey these wonderful laws of Yours" (Ps. 119:106, TLB).

That's where I often fail, but so did David at times, and like him I must say again and again, ever reminding myself, "I will obey." Consistency is a matter of the will. I will obey His laws.

I will, I will; and I'll keep reminding myself until the will in me is so conditioned and transformed that my will is to do His will, and what I will is in harmony with what He wants and what He expects me to do. That is not "mind control"; that's wanting and seeing God's control determinedly.

Some of our failures are so obvious because as we grow in faith we come into more and more of God's light, and by that light we see more of the dark corners of our lives, including the inconsistencies. Light illuminates; more light illumines more.

Because we try to be consistent every day and because we are not very successful at it, we risk the pointed finger of Satan who keeps looking at our shortcomings. Paul wrestled with that. He said: "I do not understand my own actions. For I do not do what I want, but I do the very thing I hate" (Rom. 7:15, RSV).

We need to gain perspective and see more than our failures. Otherwise what isn't the best in our lives will seem like the worst, but it really isn't—it just is not yet best.

The Process of the Work of God

Consistency, which will never completely happen this side of heaven, is possible to a large degree if we learn to enjoy the process of the work of God in our lives. Growing, with all of its setbacks, sensitizes us to God's action in us. We don't have to be always thinking about where we are not; we can rejoice at where we are. Five-year-olds always want to be six, but they don't let that stop them from the enjoyment of being five. They still run and play and do things that five-year-olds do. We can also learn to "be" right as we are, where we are.

Learn to pray, to commit your priorities over and over again to God—your failures too. We are assured, "If we confess our sins, He is faithful and just to forgive us our sins" (1 John 1:9). Learn to laugh at yourself—even when you fall flat on your face. Sometimes we think laughter is a product of our good feelings about something, but often it comes from looking at a situation and understanding it.

A man I know finds it increasingly difficult to laugh because he sees his failures in the pursuit of his priorities. Money is serious business to him, children are a worry, the world situation is troubling, and his health is not so good. Doctors know that the Bible is true when it states: "A merry heart doeth good like a medicine: but a broken spirit drieth the bones" (Prov. 17:22). Learn to relax in your "failures"; God knows you want to be consistent. He knows your struggle. He has more invested in this business of faithfulness than you have. His name is on the line—He owns you.

It is easy to give up on consistency. Many people start well but do not hold on for the long haul. The patient plodder is consistent and will still be going on while the impatient ones have stopped or gone off in other directions.

The people who steadily do something with their lives are those who endure setbacks, hardships, and defeats. But they still press on. No one has to prod them; they themselves have a "carry-through" quality; they are consistent. Few among us have that quality, but we all need it. Those who work at consistency will be the ones in whom God will invest more of Himself, and they will do God's work.

Consistency means going on, no matter what the times bring. Are you without a job? You won't always be; keep trying. Take anything, but keep going. Are you in poor health? Go on with what health you have. Many times we are inspired by the productive lives of those who are sick or paralyzed.

One afternoon as I watched the runners in the Boston Marathon, the ones who impressed me most were not the lithe, swift, and sinuous athletes but rather the men and women in wheelchairs who went the whole distance, including Heartbreak Hill.

Some of us lament our luck. We dwell on what might have occurred for us or what should have been done for us. The wheelchair marathoners didn't do that. They just practiced and practiced, and on the day of the race they went the distance. They weren't quitters because of handicaps; neither should Christians be quitters.

Don't be discouraged by what appears to be slow growth. In the long run, it is the best growth. It allows you to assimilate truth as you go. Remember that flashy growth is like the seeds planted on stony ground that Jesus described in the parable in Mark 4. They spring up quickly in shallow soil, but they don't make it over the long, hot summer.

A careful builder places brick upon brick—consistently using his level, for if he neglects the care of one brick, it will weaken the whole wall. Students know that they must take prerequisite courses that are not always what they would like to take in order to be able to take the courses in their major field of study. God wants to train His children precept upon precept, line upon line (Isa. 28:10), to bring us to maturity. His precepts are ours to build with, consistently—little by little by little.

Follow-through in our growth means being steady, an ongoing effort that must be central if there is to be personal consistency to help us reach our goals. Great skyscrapers aren't built by the dreams of the architects, but without those dreams the buildings would never begin. Men and women aren't led to faith in Christ by neat slogans or quick encounters—they are prayed for, loved, and brought along step by step. The dream is always there; it is fulfilled by consistency. Persistence, faithfulness, continuation, make the difference in how we live and how much we accomplish in our lives. The difference will show in victories won, goals accomplished, and priorities fulfilled.

Decide now to renew your promise to God to be faithful and consistent. Or if you never promised, promise now.

Live by Faith, Not Fear

Because God cares about you and is working with you, you can anticipate results. Even if those results are never all that you would wish for, they are more than you would ever have without Him. God is working; He has plans for you.

Beware of your inconsistencies, but don't be afraid of them. Fear can cripple you. You are to live by faith, not fear. "For ye have not received the spirit of bondage again to fear; but ye have received the Spirit of adoption, whereby we cry, 'Abba, Father' " (Rom. 8:15). You are adopted. You may be a weak, failing, stumbling child, but you are His child.

Always pay attention to what you are doing. That's one of the keys to consistency. You will succeed in the big things if you pay attention to the little details. Are you attentive to what people are saying? Are you attentive to what you read? Are you attentive to the scriptural truths that you are taking in each day in your Bible reading? Are you applying these truths to your life? Are you paying attention to your work habits, your ethics, your tongue? If you are working at consistency even in your private times, you will also be faithful in your public times.

God sees you all the time. The psalmist cried, "O Lord, You have searched me and You know me. You know when I sit and when I rise; You perceive my thoughts from afar. You discern my going out and my lying down; You are familiar with all my ways" (Ps. 139:1-3, NIV). What others see in public, God has already seen in private.

If you are going to be consistent every day, you have to think a lot about yourself. That's different than thinking highly of yourself or promoting yourself, though all of us do some of that too. Focus on yourself. Think about your likes, your dislikes, the patterns that you follow, so that your priorities fit in with who you are and what you are. A consistent system of priority living will come out of your personality, your skills, your talents, all of which are part of your personal makeup. You can't pretend or try to be somebody else. You can't live in conflict with yourself.

Consistently You

What you are is going to be consistently "you" every day. You always live in contact with yourself. The pattern of living out your priorities will fit that self. In short, consistency means you are not living in opposition to yourself. You are not copying other people or playacting—that's what children do. It is their way of discovery. But by the time a person becomes an adult, most of those discoveries should have been made. You are no longer trying to be "just like the boss," or "just like that teacher," or "just like Mother"; you are no longer trying "to make Dad pleased with me." You become your own person.

You are God's person—God-designed. You are your own self, by God's intention, so that you can do something with yourself that is uniquely and particularly you. You become most wholly yourself when you present yourself to God as your Creator, the source of your wisdom. You become more truly yourself when you respond to the wooing of God and transfer your trust from yourself to Jesus Christ. You become more completely yourself when you seek to obey the directions so clearly presented in Scripture. Your self will develop better when you seek a Christ-exalting body of believers whose counsel and advice to you will be centered in the authority of God's Word.

Taking these steps is an act of maturity. Such self-presentation to God is a definite step in commitment that is best for you, best for others, best for the world, and best for the kingdom of God. At last you will be "in sync" with reality. At last, as God's person, you will have what it takes to have a full, rewarding, consistent life.

Thoughtfully Aware

Those who teach "success techniques" often tell us that we need to take our eyes off other people and be inner-directed, and that is true. Of all the people on this earth, Christians probably do that best. They are inner-directed. But they are not inner-directed in the same way that the "success technique" people teach. Christians are directed from within because within them is the Spirit of God. Believers, having presented themselves to the living God, open up their minds, their souls, their hearts—their very beings—to God. They are a chosen, guarded and preserved people; they have life, purpose, and direction.

As Christians, we are aware that Christ is our strength, and that the Holy Spirit is our positive influence. We are daily strengthened inside as we walk with God. If it is true of anybody, it is true of believers: we know where our strength comes from. We know who gives it. We know that our minds are renewed day by day. We know who removes the negatives—the sin—from our lives and replaces them with the clean, the beautiful, and the pure. We know who fills us with Himself. We know the One to whom we belong.

Consistency means we are always seeking to learn more about ourselves, more about other people, and more about our surroundings, so that we can live well the life that God has given us. The truth of learning, of course, is that the more we learn, the more we realize we don't know. However, the less we learn, the more we usually think we know. And we govern our opinions by our foolishness. The quiet learner, the consistent believer, has a storehouse of wisdom on which to draw, and that storehouse is always full. No matter how much we use there is more.

In the consistency of following your priorities, be a consistent learner. It will influence every aspect of your life.

Safeguards to Protect

The consistent learner has safeguards. He knows enough about himself and about human nature to know that he can't always trust himself. There is protection in that knowledge. Carefulness is not fearfulness. Carefulness is wisdom. "Evil pursueth sinners: but to the righteous good shall be repayed" (Prov. 13:21). Think of it, evil actually chases after sinners! And there are so many traps.

In my basement study there is a mousetrap. It is baited and set, just waiting. It sits on the bottom of one of my bookshelves in front of the section on history and philosophy. Visiting mice know nothing of history and philosophy. They aren't even aware that others of their species have stopped by that trap before and, after the sound of a loud crack, have never moved again. All the mice caught in the trap have been tempted by the little bit of peanut butter on that trap. They leave no written notes, no published works to warn others of the dangers of mousetraps or of eating peanut butter where peanut butter shouldn't be.

If those mice had stayed outdoors, they might have been safe. I have no traps set there. Food is out there too, plus liberty. I have no anger about their sharing my yard. But they have persisted in invading my study and they don't belong there.

There is a parallel between those mice and us. Where do we go when are are looking for something a little different, something enticing—a little peanut butter where it shouldn't be? What need in our lives makes us want to visit a forbidden place, to try a tempting snack? Are we as ignorant as those mice to the history of others before us who have been trapped by the same desire to satisfy some craving to be in a forbidden place?

We are all like mice unless someone teaches us a higher way than we have been teaching ourselves. Who will do that?

There is a higher wisdom, a God-given wisdom. Proverbs speaks of wisdom calling, but sin calls also, and sin uses the same words as wisdom. If we are not carefully listening, we may not hear God's wisdom call!

The Long-term Place of Abiding

One of the fruits of the Spirit is joy—not necessarily a quickly springing-up joy such as the seed planted in the stony ground, but a mature joy that comes from a full summer of abiding in the Vine. Settle into the long-term place of abiding. When fruit bearing comes, that fruit will include joy.

David sang, "One thing have I desired of the Lord, that will I seek after; that I may dwell in the house of the Lord all the days of my life, to behold the beauty of the Lord, and to inquire in His temple" (Ps. 27:4). We need to *dwell* with God.

I recently met a man who always wanted to be a full-time Christian worker. Yet circumstances forced this man as a young teen to quit school and go to work. Today he is experiencing genuine happiness through working with Christian organizations. God has given him large sums of money, and this is used for the Lord's work. He can point to examples of how God has led in his life, and he is a joy to know. He follows God consistently, not in the way he would have chosen himself but in the way God chose for him.

He is a wise man; he gets his priorities from God. In obedience to those priorities and to God who gave them, he is consistent every day. Under the daily leading of God, we can be consistent too.

Giving God a Chance with Me

7

It was past midnight when our telephone rang. Glenn, a seminary student, was calling from his home. He was distraught. "I'm worn out," he said. "Pray for me." And he started to cry. He had been trying to work extra hours at his church, study for exams, and help other students with their problems. The "too many" late nights had finally caught up with him.

After some counseling and prayer, Glenn agreed that he was doing too much. He was reminded of what Paul Little used to tell students at the Inter-Varsity missionary conventions at Urbana: "There is nothing unspiritual about sleep."

Two months later Glenn wrote to say that he was feeling better. "I've scheduled some 'do nothing' time and I'm sticking to it."

Jesus took time to turn aside, to rest and pray even when people were crowding Him, demanding His time and energy. When there was too much to do, He went off to be alone with His Father (cf. Matt. 14:22-23). Every believer should take notes on how and when Jesus did it. In fact, we need to copy Jesus lest we start to think that we are different from those whom He told, "The disciple is not above his master, nor the servant above his lord" (Matt. 10:24).

Yes to Ourselves

Having established and listed your priorities, having analyzed your short-term and long-term goals, and having committed yourself to pressing on, are you moving past the slavish keeping of those priorities to relaxed living in Christ? Do your priorities and your commitment to them allow for down time, alone time, reading time, laughing time, vacation time, and memory-building time?

I know a couple who are reaching the point where they soon may resent God. They're in a church that demands activity. Both husband and wife work because the economy makes it difficult for them to get along on one paycheck. Both feel driven to serve on church boards, and to be present whenever the church doors are open. They are pressed to give more and more of their money to the church because of expansion of facilities and programs. He teaches a Sunday School class, and they feel obliged to counsel people who have problems.

There is almost a love/hate relationship going: they want to serve the church because Christ loved the church and gave Himself for it and they feel that they must do no less; they want to be available to people because they care for them in the Lord. But when the phone rings they can feel their anger building up inside: *Why don't they leave us alone?*

These people don't know how to say no. Many of us are just like them. We don't know how to say no at work, in the community, to friends, or to church responsibilities. We add more and more to our schedules, feeling guilty if we are not doing more, yet beginning to wonder if this is what the Christian life is all about.

One of the reasons for being free to say no to others is to be able to say yes to ourselves. I remember a man who one evening said to his guests, "You can stay as long as you want to, but I am going to bed." He was not a night person; he needed his rest. He went to bed and we let ourselves out when we were ready to leave.

I heard another man say, "If you will excuse me, I have some things to do before I go to bed."

A few days later I asked him, "What were those things you had to do before you went to bed?"

He smiled and said, "I had to brush my teeth and wash my face and put on my pajamas."

I saw his point. We cannot let others own our time. We don't do them any favors if they dictate our schedules, and we don't do ourselves any favors either—not if we are going to be faithful to God and have something left to give others.

That doesn't mean that we are to be so selfish that we are unbending. Of course there are times when we should do things for others, when we can't just stick to our own schedules. We have certain obligations. Work is one, family is one, church is another, community is another—and we must fit them in. But we can't achieve our goals by always allowing others to fit us into their schedules.

Being able to say no to others is possible when we are able to say yes to ourselves. We are better able to serve others and God if we are not always being run by the schedules of other people and not always needing to be "needed" every waking minute. That frees us to usher out a houseful of guests in order to put our slippered feet up and have a half hour of quiet time with the Lord to restore our soul. No one but God can restore my soul for me.

How often do we hear people say, "Well, I suppose I can do that; I was only going to sit home and read that night anyway." Maybe before the Lord and in faithfulness to Him they should sit home and read that night and not do the proposed project. Maybe that's the only night they have to collect their thoughts, renew their strength, and seek the mind of God. Maybe exhaustion is not necessarily a Christian virtue. Maybe we have fallen for the teaching that busyness is Christian, and that quietness and renewal is not. Maybe we are raising our children to believe that the Christian way is the activity way—always doing. And maybe we have been wrong. God says, "In quietness and in confidence shall be your strength" (Isa. 30:15).

Time Is a Commodity

Who runs your life? If you have no plan, everyone else will make your plans for you. If others fill up your hours, you will come to resent people. But if you give to others out of your own desire to give, you will enjoy it. Time is a commodity—it is from God. You don't let other people spend your money, you decide how it is going to be spent. You don't let others raise your children, you do it. Why then do you scatter your time before others as if they are free to spend it as they wish? You have an obligation before God to give your time to other people as a gift—just as you give money as a gift—not to have it taken from you. Robbery is not Christian; giving is Christian.

You are not more holy for all of your giving up of yourself. You are to give up yourself only to God who rules you. But you will respond to people in obedience as God sends them. In times of prayer, you sense God's leading and want to help others even if it sometimes means leaving your family dinner table or staying up all night to help somebody. You do this ministry out of your wholeness, not because of the demands of others. Being used is not Christian. Christians give themselves away. Giving ourselves is a theological stand. Some of us are trying to live a life of faith not by faith at all but by earning merit through work.

You are saved by faith. Absolutely nothing you can do

makes you acceptable to God. "Not by works of righteousness which we have done, but according to His mercy He saved us" (Titus 3:5). You come with an open heart to God confessing your sins, relying totally on the work that God did through Jesus Christ in His death and resurrection.

The Holy Spirit brought you to faith, showed you your need, and convinced you of your lost condition and your need for the Saviour. That same Holy Spirit is living within you right now, helping and guiding you.

Yet we think that we must do everything ourselves, saying, "God has no hands but our hands." We feel that the salvation of the world is our responsibility. We feel great guilt over people we have not yet witnessed to. We say, "God is waiting for us to act."

But maybe we are wrong. Maybe God is saying to us, "Wait a minute. I am God apart from you; you need Me." In all of your running around, when do you do your thinking? When do you do your praying? When do you do absolutely nothing else but reflect on the goodness and mercy of God?

Part of Your Soul

When do you talk to your spouse and children about things other than problems—especially church problems? When do you talk about the lessons of God?

For whom do you pray? Who prays for you? When do you have time for God to get close to you?

What is God's first and overriding commandment? It is found in Deuteronomy 6:5: "Thou shalt love the Lord thy God with all thine heart, and with all thy soul, and with all thy might."

Are you to love God with part of your heart? No! With the rest of your heart being elsewhere? No!

Does the Scripture say part of your soul? Just a small portion of your might? Or all of it? We are to love God with our total being.

The closest example we have of this kind of love is the love we have for our spouses. When do you best love your spouse? When you're at work, engaged in solving some business problem? Do you love best in the community when you are involved in some activity? Is it when you are in church serving on a board? Or is it when you're at home together and quiet and not focusing on anything else but each other? When two people fall out of love, it is because they have worked at it—they worked at doing everything except being together.

When do you have your together time with God? When do you have time to love Him and for Him to love you? You don't rush through it; you don't love Him in activity. You love Him when you're together. You love God best when you can talk together and be together.

Deuteronomy 6:6 says, "You must think constantly about these commandments" (TLB) or, as another translation puts it, "These words . . . shall be on your heart" (NASB). When His commands are on your heart, when you are thinking about them constantly, then you can teach them to your children (v. 7). It doesn't say teach them to your children as abstract philosophical ideas, but teach what is already in your heart. Getting His Word into your heart takes time!

We're talking about personal time—God-accessible time. If you don't have time with God first, you will have no ministry anywhere, with anyone.

The Bible says, "All Scripture is given by inspiration of God, and is profitable for doctrine, for reproof, for correction, for instruction in righteousness; that the man of God may be perfect, thoroughly furnished unto all good works" (2 Tim. 3:16). That means God's Word is given not generally, but particularly for our instruction, for our reproof, for our correction, that we may be perfect. God wants it for us—and that instruction, reproof, and correction takes time. Taking this time is not laziness but just the opposite. It is a recognition that God is Lord and He equips us for His work.

Coming and Going

Firm commands are given in Scripture to go into all the world and preach the Gospel. We are to go, teach, preach, and make disciples. We are told that the fields are white unto harvest. Discipleship is a life of commitment; more than doing Christian activities, it is a calling. We don't just take Jesus into our hearts, but we are called to obey Him. That obedience involves all that we are, all that we do; it means faithfulness to His challenge to "go . . . into all the world" (Mark 16:15). But that commitment does not mean living an exhausting life. Jesus, who called us to labor, is also the One who tells us to come apart and rest a while (cf. Mark 6:31).

This may not be a good verse to stress to anyone who may be looking in the Bible for an excuse to do what he has always wanted to do—nothing. Some people look for reasons not to do God's work. But committed Christians are active, faithful, obedient servants of God, and they must be told not to do more. We need to be reminded of all that there is in Scripture—both the commands to go and the commands to rest.

When Jesus recommended rest, there were people coming and going so constantly that Jesus and His disciples had no leisure even to eat. It may be like that for you: much coming and going with no time to eat. When that happens, instead of accomplishing more, you become irritated when one more person puts demands on you. You may also become irritated with God.

Jesus told us to rest a while. He knows what is happening to us in our rushing. If He knows when a sparrow falls, if He knows the number of hairs on our heads, then He also knows what is happening to us when we are under pressure. He had compassion on the crowds (Mark 6:34). He knew their needs. He cared about them. He insisted that people be fed, but He also knew the value of getting away and resting a while. He chose a lonely place, leaving the crowds. If we are going to rest, gain perspective, be fed by the Spirit of God, and get our priorities in order, we have to do that too.

Jesus isn't telling us not to care; all scriptural evidence is otherwise. He isn't telling us to ignore people, quite the opposite. But He is saying, "Let's go off alone for a while." We need time with Jesus.

When did you last have a vacation with just your family? When did you last sit home in the evening instead of rushing off to some club or social event, or even to another church meeting? When did you last go aside to rest a while? Even a machine has to be shut down to be cleaned and oiled. As much as there is a danger of sloth and laziness in some people, there is the serious danger of overwork—adrenaline-pumping, heart-racing, ulcer-producing pressure in others. And we break down. Our necks and shoulders ache. Our heads hurt. Our bodies get tired. We can't make it; we can't go on. It is time to rest.

Pushing on is foolish. It destroys the beautiful body machine that God created, and we cannot, if we worship God the Creator, disregard the body that He made. The psalmist cried: "Have mercy upon me, O Lord, for I am in trouble; mine eye is consumed with grief, yea, my soul and my belly" (Ps. 31:9).

If we are sick physically or mentally, it will affect us spiritually. When our bodies waste away, so does our spirit. We become dry spiritually and we no longer operate in a balanced way. God rested from His creating work on the seventh day. Surely He did so not because He was weak but because it is as much a part of the nature of God as consistency, faithfulness, and goodness. He was teaching a lesson. God rests, and so should those who follow Him.

In the pursuit of priority living—accomplishing goals and redeeming the time—we need quiet time. Workers often joke that on Monday mornings they always feel tired. Someone quipped, "Monday is an awful way to spend one-seventh of our lives." We wear ourselves out over the weekend, even on the day of rest.

People often return from vacations more exhausted than they were before they started out. They come back to rest up. That's not good discipline. Maybe instead of seeing ten lakes and five mountains, we need to sit and absorb just one lake or mountain and let it sink into our consciousness for peace and therapy. There is spiritual renewal in doing so. "Learn of Me," the Master tells us (Matt. 11:29).

God Visits in the Quiet

One afternoon, during a tour of Israel with fellow journalists, we were in Sinai for a visit to the Monastery Santa Katarina. The monks were taking us through the library and the "storage" rooms where all the skulls and bones of ancient monks are kept. I was tired. The trip had been hectic and busy. I wanted to be alone. So I slipped away from the group and went out through the garden wall. I walked a few hundred feet out into the desert. And there, with my back against a warm rock, I sat looking at Mount Sinai, just letting it become a part of me, soaking it all in, fixing it in my mind.

I thought about Moses and other people throughout history who walked over the rocks in Sinai. I thought about all that God did for His people there. But for a time I just sat, letting the whole feeling of what was there become a part of me. I didn't take photographs of the mountain. I didn't run here or there to get a better view. I just sat. A bedouin boy came along with a goat, but seeing me he made a wide berth and kept going. After about a half hour, I returned to the group, I was rested, peaceful, not harried, and had in my subconscious a sense of the sights, the feeling, the warmth, the smell of Sinai. It is still with me. I can close my eyes and be mentally transported back there. I would have missed that if I had merely been a busy tourist.

I am not a great fisherman. But once a year I like to take five days and go to a lake, sit out in a boat in the middle of that lake, and fish. I don't always catch fish. But it is quiet. I am alone. I watch the birds and listen to the lake sounds; I let the quietness do its healing. It is therapy for me. I have even sat out alone in the rain, knowing that a week later I would be back on a full work schedule. I am renewing my strength. And in the quiet, God visits with me.

I have renewal times at home too. We live in a city, but there are restful places to walk. I know where there is a little duck pond and I watch the ducks. By the end of the summer I have come to know them and their offspring. They disappear when winter comes. In winter I walk other places. I go to a park where children take their sleds and teenagers play hockey. I see all kinds of things when I am walking. It is exercise, but it is also mentally peaceful. Winter nights, especially when the temperature is below zero, are quiet nights. I'm bundled warmly, the streets are still, and I'm alone with God.

I need a time for renewal, a time to seek God, a time to pray. I find new direction in these times. I work too many long hours, have too many heavy assignments, not to take time to retreat. This is a priority. I need to give God a chance to renew me.

Is God less happy with us when we are quiet and alone than when we are preaching, or teaching, or witnessing, or writing? Do we honor Him less?

A Delightful Experience

Knowing and following Jesus is a delightful experience. It is a joy, not a misery. It is a calling that touches all of life.

There are days when we cannot say with Paul, "Rejoice in the Lord alway, and again I say, Rejoice" (Phil. 4:4). We cannot always say with the psalmist, "My heart and my flesh sing for joy to the living God" (Ps. 84:2, NASB). Christians are not always happy. We are not always full of excitement. We are not always eager to pray, or to go to Christian meetings, or to witness. The Bible is not always exciting to read. There are even days when we don't want to read it at all.

But many of us won't admit to having these feelings. If we do admit that the "joy of the Lord" is not always surrounding us, dear saints are always nearby to tell us about our spiritual problems. And there may be reasons for our lack of joy—sin in our lives, overtiredness, rundown bodies. Or our loss of spiritual balance may result from putting out far more than we are taking in spiritually. We may need forgiveness for running around too much. We may need the discipline of prayer. We may need to rest, or take a vacation. We may need laughter and play to put our lives back into balance. Jesus knows that. Come aside and rest a while: spiritually, emotionally, and physically. Rest with Him.

We have to come to the point where we don't "need" anything but God. Does that sound strange? We talk of needs, but maybe our greatest need is "not to need"—not to need more money, not to need more things, not to need more activity, not to need more fame or acclaim or even more experiences. Maybe, in Christ, we just need to be. As I am writing this I glance out the window and see a squirrel running up a tree and a robin on the ground. Why did God send them into my line of vision? Are they not there for me even as they are busy about their own affairs? They are a respite, a momentary break, a pleasure to see—a gift from God.

I look a little longer and enjoy seeing the touch of the wind on the evergreens as the branches dance and show the different sides of their fernlike stems. I watch the sky; it is a gray day. The sun is up there somewhere, although I can't see it. But I can enjoy the mixed weather, for that is mine too. God gives little pleasure breaks in routine—detours—and they are good. I find myself smiling, laughing, and saying "thank You" as He gives these gifts. These surprises come all day long. God gives these—but so many people miss them. They can't enjoy God's gifts; they think they need to be out and doing.

I have been reading some of the writings of the philosopher Ludwig Wittgenstein, a study of his explanation of language. He writes of "responsible" language; that is, language pertaining to life as we know it and can measure it; and of language that is "non" sense because it pertains to the unmeasurable, such as faith and love. How does reading Wittgenstein help me? I don't know; maybe it won't help me at all immediately. Yet in the economy of God I know that all that I read and study comes together in my mind and is helpful. Education is not always immediately utilitarian. It is growth, pleasant growth. That's God's gift too.

Gathering interesting insights from the mind of another person helps me. It doesn't have to have an immediate meaning to have value. The same is true of music and art. God gives the talents that produce them, and ears and eyes to enjoy them.

As you establish and follow your priorities, don't put all the stress on doing work. Recognize that along the way God is going to give you lessons and pleasures in life. That doesn't mean to dally, to look only for pleasures along the way. Keep your eyes on your goals, but do so knowing that God can bring in detours.

It's all quite relaxing, for in God's work we don't have to determine everything for ourselves all of the time. We just have to be with Him. Along the way of priority living, always give God first chance with you.

Your Family, a Gift from God

8

It doesn't take a lot of time to build family memories. One afternoon, when our children were smaller, we decided to have a picnic. The park where we picnicked was near a large woods, so we took our dog along, a black Labrador retriever. The day was beautiful, though the sky seemed somewhat threatening as we laid out the picnic lunch on the table. Just after we sat down to eat, a thunderstorm suddenly came on us, pouring rain. Quickly, we gathered up our food, raced to our Volkswagen, and the four of us jammed inside. We spread out the food on our laps and the dashboard, and tried to finish our lunch in those cramped quarters. But we did not reckon on the dog. We thought she would be happy to stay out under a tree; she wasn't. She cried and barked and carried on because she was getting soaked. Unable to resist her pleading any longer, we opened the car door and let her in. Four people with a picnic lunch in a Volkswagen is cramped. Add to that a soggy Labrador retriever and you have a crowd. A wet dog takes over a car, and all of our food tasted like wet fur.

None of us will ever forget that picnic. It wasn't a big

expensive trip; it didn't take a long time, but it was fun. It is even more fun now as we remember it and laugh.

A Priority Time

You who have young families, decide now whether you're going to focus on a nice home and a boat and two cars, or making your priority happy kids. Are nice clothes and other things going to be more important or will time with your children rate first? Society has set its priorities about home life; now you have to set yours.

When your children grow up, are they going to remember that Dad worked two jobs or that Dad helped them repair their bicycles and went to Little League games with them?

Will they be able to say, "Dad was there"?

And is Mom there too? Are they going to learn how to play with their own children by the way you play with them? Are they going to learn to pray that way too?

We have Bible reading and prayer in the evening after supper. Since there are four of us, we each take a turn reading Scripture from whatever part of the Bible we are reading during our private quiet times. The readings are short and so are the prayers. We pray for people who have asked for prayer, those we know who are sick, missionaries from whom we receive letters, family situations, schoolwork, job problems, anything and everything. These are happy times. Some of our best conversations have come out of those moments discussing prayer needs. Then we each pray for the needs discussed. Family prayer time is a special time, a priority time, but it has to be a decided priority. It has to be worked at.

I wrote an article for *Decision* magazine about our family prayer life, telling how we got started and sharing little vignettes about our children's prayers when they were young. At the end of the article, I asked readers to share their experiences with family prayer. Though we receive many letters at *Decision* magazine, the response to the article was fewer than a dozen letters—and two of those were requests for help. Why didn't more people write about their family prayer times? Probably because they don't have a prayer time to write about. Many people talk about family prayer, but not many are doing it.

Christians have allowed the telephone, the children's schedules, individual daily activities, and television to interfere with what could be one of the best times of the day. We established prayer as a priority for our family before our children were born. We prayed for our children before birth; we prayed for them at birth; we have prayed for them every day since. And now they pray for us. It is a wonderful thing to be prayed for by each other in the family. Family time with God is a priority. It has to be, or it won't happen.

That doesn't mean that we have a perfect home or perfect family relationships. My kids can become sullen, and they don't always want to do what they're asked to do. They crab about things.

I crab about things. I get as worked up about problems as anybody else.

My mother-in-law requires a lot of time. The children want to talk when I want to read the paper.

I'm not a saint as a husband. My wife knows there are weeds in my garden. That's why I like to read about others who have family irritations too. I take comfort in people who are like me.

Leslie B. Flynn, in his book *You Don't Have to Go It Alone*, talks about Harry Ironside, the Bible teacher, who late one Sunday night reprimanded his wife: " 'You should not have spoken so abruptly to me. Do you realize I preached six times today?' She replied, 'Do you realize I had to listen to you six times today?' " (Accent Books, p. 74)

Dr. M.R. DeHaan, of the Radio Bible Class, told his staff one day, "This morning Mrs. DeHaan and I had a little disagreement, and I didn't say anything at all as we ate breakfast. Finally it was time to read the devotional in *Our Daily Bread.* She did so silently to herself for a moment. Then taking it and shoving it under my nose she asked, 'Are you the man who wrote this?' I read the article and felt about an inch tall. It had to do with kindness and forbearance. That did it! We had to make up right there" (Flynn, *You Don't Have to Go It Alone,* p. 83).

I'm like that. I don't hold myself up as an example. My wife and I have tried to live as Christian examples in our home. But I don't know how much our children appreciate it.

Yet God didn't make me a father in order to be appreciated. He gave me that congregation called my family and I am to be their teacher. I'm their example. As I look at the Bible listings of the fruit of the Spirit (see Gal. 5:22-23), I know what my life is supposed to be. You know what yours is to be too, in your home. Your family is your ministry—a God-given priority.

Follow Through at Home.

We are often self-conscious about what is "wrong" with us. We know that if we are going to be consistent with our priorities, that consistency had better be obvious to those nearest us—our families. They won't hear our teachings about prayer if we don't pray with them. They won't hear our words about love if we don't love them. They won't listen to us quoting Scripture if Scripture is not applied in our daily lives at home. They won't listen to our descriptions of faithful Christian living if they only see unfaithful living that is anything but Christian. If we are going to follow through any place in our priorities, we had better follow through at home. If our children are a priority, it had better be obvious to them. If your spouse is a priority, it had better be obvious.

Your spouse is your ministry too. God gave you to each other for a reason. He knew what He was doing when He selected your spouse for you and you for your spouse. Your togetherness isn't just emotional or physical or because you like the same books. Your togetherness, at its deepest level, is spiritual. Intimacy, true intimacy, is the sharing of two souls. To expose your soul, to let the other person be a part of your innermost being, is a communication of the real you. When you can offer your soul openly to God before your spouse, and your spouse can do the same, that's true biblical "knowing."

Since God ordained marriage and has brought you together, don't you think that it's because He knows your spiritual needs and because He knows your spouse's spiritual needs too? Each of you is the teacher of the other. You have been brought together to help one another. Your spouse can give you spiritual counsel and teaching, and you can do the same for your spouse. God brought you together so that you can help each other come closer to Himself where He wants you to be. That is His design! Is looking after the spiritual welfare of your spouse a priority of your life? Has activity gotten in the way of your prayer life? Has business gotten in the way of Bible reading? How can you free up your spouse to spend time with God, to read, to attend a prayer group or a church conference that will be valuable? Are there times when you should be discussing your own personal spiritual condition together and helping one another grow? Are you praying together so that your hearts meet? Can God speak to one and thus speak to both? Can God bless your spouse through you? God wants you both to be mature and growing in the faith. That's why He arranged for the two of you to complement each other. And that's why marriage is permanent. It's a spiritual investment of two persons to each other. God will bring dividends from that investment.

Your children are God's gift to you also. He selected the genes; He formed those new persons. He knows who they are going to become. He knows what He wants to do in their lives. He knows what they need in spiritual teaching. That's why He brought them to you. Don't ever renege on your responsibility as their spiritual mentor. You are their guide. You are their example. They learn about Christ as they watch you follow Him. They judge the love of the heavenly Father as they watch you. Often children respond to God—positively or negatively—on the basis of the way they respond to their parents. Referring to God's teaching, the psalmist said, "We will not hide them from their children, showing to the generation to come the praises of the Lord, and His strength, and His wonderful works that He hath done" (Ps. 78:4).

Be Spiritual Teachers

How beautiful for children to grow in such a way that they never really remember a time when they didn't believe and want to be obedient and faithful to the living Lord Christ. What a beautiful testimony to parents when young lives continue to be shaped day by day through the years, through education, through the ups and downs of life, through the struggles that come to us all. God brings those young people to maturity under the tutoring of parents who are themselves maturing in the faith. "Even a child is known by his doings, whether his work be pure, and whether it be right" (Prov. 20:11).

God has allowed you to have these visitors in your home for these training years. Love them in a way that they will want to continue to be a part of your family long after they have families of their own. Live so that as grandparents you will be allowed to be spiritual teachers to your grandchildren, even as you continue to be quietly available to your children. Live so that they all will know that you are praying for them and that you will continue to do so on through the generations for as long as God gives you breath. God yearns for obedience and faithfulness to Him. "O that there were such an heart in them, that they would fear Me, and keep all My commandments always, that it might be well with them, and with their children forever!" (Deut. 5:29) Your obedience to God's commands matters not only for your own lifetime but for the generations that follow.

Think of the dynasties, the generations of great Christian leaders you know about. "Children are an heritage of the Lord" (Ps. 127:3). For generations to come, children will rise up and call blessed those parents who have been faithful.

But we cannot organize our families' lives any more than we can organize our friends' lives. There has to be acceptance and trust. We never stop praying. In fact, most godly parents know that the more they loosen the apron strings, the more time they seem to spend in prayer. But we have to learn that ultimately it is God to whom our children must answer, not to us or our expectations.

On a visit to Harvard University, I admired the lovely ivy that covers the walls of some of the buildings. The next day I read in *The Harvard Crimson* that the ivy was destroying the walls. There were arguments about keeping the ivy or taking it down. Beauty, if it clings too tightly, can destroy.

A close family is a beautiful thing. Children can be a complement to their parents and bring praise. But parents, by holding on too long to what adds beauty to their lives, can destroy the structure of that relationship. Make letting go a priority. Pray about how and when to do it so that you will be neither too early nor too late. Children are not necessarily equipped to decide that time for themselves (some children who scream the loudest about being grown-up are the least grown-up). Parents must decide how much independence to give their children in the light of each child's maturity, needs, and personality. Make the decision prayerfully and in love. Some parents never make that decision and discover at great pain that they have hurt their children—maybe even lost them.

"Family" Doesn't Just Happen

Many couples are working quietly and carefully for the preservation of marriage, the institution that God established. They are teaching their children about the commitment of marriage. The security of marriage and home is a priority to them because they have made it a priority. Millions of believers know that "family" doesn't just happen; there has been a conscious decision that it will happen. We commit ourselves to the family day after day after day. We work at it. We keep communication lines as open as we can. We decide that there is no back door—no escape clause in marriage or family. We are committed for better or for worse, and we will build a strong home.

God honors that commitment. He always has. A lustful, pleasure-seeking "I want" attitude can destroy the home. Disciplined people who make a priority of marriage solidarity will not be caught in that selfish trap. They make the decision that they must follow the laws of God on marriage and family, not because they are more spiritual than somebody else but because they refuse to make light of their commitment, and refuse to break their vow before God. They made a promise to God when they married, a promise to God when they committed each baby to Him. They are determined, by the strength and grace given by God, that their promises will be kept.

Our self-denial, our commitment to marriage, our faithfulness before God as husband and wife are some of the best ways of teaching our children what marriage is all about. How else will they know what God designed? Certainly they will not find that design in their reading, or in films, or on television, or in school. They must see it at home as they watch their parents.

You can't have a growing marriage unless you have a living marriage. You can't have life unless you have come to the One who is Life. A Christian marriage is indeed a true, vital, and vibrant relationship because it is God's doing and God is in it. That's why Christian marriage is so exceptional, and that is why Satan tries so hard to disrupt it.

What Strange Teaching

Those who are "crucified with Christ" (see Gal. 2:20) are best equipped for marriage. Two crucified selves, alive in Christ and in the joy of the Lord, can and will work together in Christ by the power of the Holy Spirit. The direction of the Lord will build their life together because they have decided to allow the Word (written and living) to guide, influence, and fill their lives. They have been transformed by the renewing of their minds. They are daily proving "what is that good, and acceptable, and perfect, will of God" (Rom. 12:2).

Because of the priority of their commitment to God, and the priority of the family, a Christian couple should never bring up the word "divorce." Their vocabulary for building shouldn't include words for destruction. They should focus on the beauty and the harmony and the good that can come out of building together, working together not to hurt but to help.

Some will say, "What strange teaching." But it only seems strange because it is so uncommon to hear. We are living in a time when the normal sounds abnormal. Yet, deep down inside, believers know that commitment is normal, and unbelievers suspect that it is also.

What will your children see at home? Will they see what the Apostle Paul explained:

Love is patient, love is kind. It does not envy, it does not boast, it is not proud. It is not rude, it is not self-seeking, it is not easily angered, it keeps no record of wrongs. Love does not delight in evil but rejoices with the truth. It always protects, always trusts, always hopes, always perseveres (1 Cor. 13:4-7, NIV).

Is that kind of love at your house? We applaud the great preachers who teach thousands; we applaud the great administrators who guide large organizations; we applaud the corporate businessmen who can earn large sums of money for their companies; we applaud the statesmen who can bring nations together in peace. Isn't it time to applaud the men and women who, through discipline and care and Christian obedience, have established and built solid homes on the love of Christ Jesus and who are teaching the fullness of all that love means to generations to come? These are the true leaders in our world; they are God's leaders. They practice what they teach every day when all around them there is neither the practice nor the teaching. They have kept going against great odds, and they are winning.

As you live each day with your family, remember that what counts is neither yesterday nor tomorrow; what matters is now. This is the day to enjoy one another, to encourage one another, to teach, to discipline if necessary, and above all to love one another. "This is the day which the Lord hath made" (Ps. 118:24).

Life Is Now

Unfortunately, there is a tendency to think more about what we did as a family last week or about what we will do next month, than we do about the present. Life is now, not only for our children, but for our parents, and for our grandparents too. That little word spoken in tenderness can't be saved until someone is in the hospital. Our helping hand, our guidance, is important now—not after we have reached a certain earning level or have purchased a larger house. Now is the time to live as a family. Memories tomorrow come from living today.

All of us have regrets about the things we didn't do. Parents can think of a thousand ways that they might have done things differently. There are tears. And children, remembering some of their own ways, can go through the same torture after their parents are gone.

Children are instructed to honor their parents, and that is an obligation no matter how their parents behave. "Honor thy father and mother" (Ex. 20:12). In our parents' old age we may have to care for them, support them, even endure abuse from them—but honor them we must; that is not an option. This command has a promise attached to it: "that thy days may be long" (Ex. 20:12). Does this literally mean that we will live longer? If we don't honor our parents, will our lives be cut short? Think about that!

Are you honoring your parents? Maybe they are not honorable people, but the Bible gives the command: "Honor your parents." If we can't honor our parents whom we see, how can we honor God whom we have not seen? If we cannot take the responsibility for those who need us as they grow old, how can we be trusted to take responsibility for anybody? Our parents, like our children, may have little to offer—unless you count love and caring and community.

We are to be responsible for our parents regardless of how they act or what they do. Our responsibility is before God, just as our parents had a responsibility before God to take care of us when we were helpless, demanding infants who kept them awake in the night. A time comes when the role is reversed, and many children experience hardships and pain, physically and emotionally, because they have selfishly refused their responsibility to honor their mother and father and to care for them.

We need to see the family as a gift from God to cherish and to love—yes, sometimes to endure—in all seasons, at all times. There is no promise of a better day. God has given us to each other *now*.

Children Aren't Projects

Some psychologists ask, "Why do we need so many programs and steps and teaching methods for raising children? Why can't we just be natural, just be together and grow?"

Well, why not? Why not let gardens be natural? Why "train up a child"? That sounds like obedience school. This view is wrong, of course, for obvious reasons. The garden is best when weeded. A dog or horse is useless if never taught or disciplined. "The rod and reproof give wisdom; but a child left to himself bringeth his mother to shame" (Prov. 29:15). Yet there is a point to what some child psychologists are saying.

Sometimes in our efforts to "train up" children, we tend to try to "build" them. We study methods, take classes, read books, seek more and more help, and become something less than flesh-and-blood parents; we look at our children much as we look at a house under construction. We stand back and inspect, then go back to the plans, then hammer some more. Children aren't projects to be completed, like houses to be finished. Often we work too hard trying to create the "perfect" child. Why can't we be less conscious of ourselves, less worried about how we shape and mold and influence them? Why do we believe that all we need are better books to tell us what to do and then other books to tell us how to alleviate our guilt if a child "turns out bad"?

We joke about children growing up in spite of us, and we know that is probably more true than we care to admit. Maybe what our children need to see most of all is that our priorities for living are just that—our priorities under God—so that they can copy, absorb, learn from, and practice, just as a baby robin learns from his mother how to dig for worms. I don't think mother robin frets too much about, "Am I doing it right?" / "Should I spend more or less time with Junior?" She doesn't try to define her role as a parent. She does what birds always do, and the little birds catch on.

We are so conscious of ourselves, so self-conscious about our parenting, so aware of our failures, and so envious of another's success, that we can't be relaxed people, let alone parents. Maybe the best priority we can set for ourselves as parents is to set priorities as people of God. Our children will get the idea.

We can't go too far into selfishness if our first priority is to praise and worship and obey God. We won't reject our children if we understand how much we are accepted. We will know security and be able to give it. Following our heavenly Father closely will make us the kind of earthly parents who are worth following—and being around. God will help us be the best parents that we can be.

My Priorities Show—to Everyone

9

I don't work on Sundays; at least I don't when I control the time. When I'm traveling, then I have to work, and Sunday is like any other day. But when I'm home, I don't work on Sunday. That's a priority.

I work hard on Saturday in order to have Sunday as a day of rest; I need it.

I need Sunday for worship. I can't be comfortable rushing to church or squeezing worship into a tight schedule.

I need Sunday for a Sunday School class whether I'm a pupil or the teacher.

I need Sunday to take a nap on Sunday afternoon.

I need Sunday to be with my family.

A man who works for an airline once challenged me: "Do you mean that I should stay home too?" No, he has to work on Sunday because people fly on Sunday. But because I don't have to work on Sunday, I won't do it. There is a difference between requirement and choice. I need a day to focus on God with no other thing interfering.

But I'm not rigid about it. I eat bread on Monday even

though I know it was baked on Sunday. My daughter sometimes works on Sunday afternoons in a restaurant. Should she work? She is feeding a lot of Christians who don't work on Sunday either but who want somebody else to work so that they can have their Sunday dinner in a restaurant. My son sometimes works at a sports arena on Sunday, serving those who want to go to sports events or concerts on Sunday evening.

But I have my own rule and it is a rule that my neighbors know. They know it not because I talk about it but because they don't see me cutting grass, or washing the car, or going into a grocery store on Sunday. It creates a quiet witness.

But I have helped neighbors who have been working and needed help on Sunday. If I see them struggling with something, I lend a hand. I can because I am not busy doing my own work. I guess it's an example of a neighbor's ox falling into a ditch (cf. Luke 14:5).

Sunday rest and worship is a priority. Some say they can worship and still paint the fence. I can't. I need a day apart. I appreciate God's rule, "Six days shalt thou labor" (Ex. 20:9). I find that I work hard on the six days, looking forward to a day when I'll have a minivacation, a day of rest. Many people who feel they need Sunday to accomplish needed work probably spread out their six days' work into seven because they know they have that day to work. I don't "have" that day. I don't expect it. Sunday is a worship day, a day of rest—that's a priority.

Be Positive Neighbors

Another priority I have is to be a witness in our community. Each summer our neighborhood has a block party. Some years that means contributing to the fund for a beer keg. My wife and I have two choices—we can object and create a fuss or put in our money, be friendly to our neighbors, and drink ginger ale.

We try to attend the school meetings or community meetings on rezoning, and we try to be involved positively in local elections. We helped a woman on our street campaign for a city office. She lost, but we were out with the other neighbors distributing fliers.

We try to be positive neighbors; that's a priority. But we also say no when we cannot go along biblically. We will not let the community dictate our priorities.

We say no on our terms, in order to be able to grow quietly in the Lord. We don't do it in arrogance; we aren't nasty to the neighbors. In fact, we are more and more conscious of the need to be loving because arrogance is a problem among Christians, and Christians make the news in a negative way when they are arrogant. Some of us as Christians have forgotten that it is God who is truth, not our opinions. We have forgotten that the Bible is inspired, but our personal theology is not.

I remember while visiting Oslo, Norway seeing marchers with signs stating, "Give Christians power and they will kill you." I smiled then, thinking, "Surely they can't be serious." But a couple of years later, during a conference for Christians in Kansas City, a newspaper reporter asked with some concern, "My city has many Jewish and Muslim people in it. With all of you evangelicals trying to convert people, are Jews and Muslims going to be safe on the streets?" Then I realized that some people are afraid of us. Because of what they read or hear, some people assume that we're no different than the religious fundamentalists in Muslim countries, and they are afraid of us. They see militant fundamentalism. They don't know that real Christians follow the God of love. The best priority we can practice daily in our communities is to live out quietly and lovingly the life we have in Christ.

People don't see much real love among their friends or in their homes. They are looking for a contrast, and if they see that contrast in us, they'll ask what makes us different. We need to be ready for that question in our communities. Scripture says, "Sanctify the Lord God in your hearts; and be ready always to give an answer to every man that asketh you a reason of the hope that is in you with meekness and fear" (1 Peter 3:15). First we sanctify, then we are ready to give a reason.

What we are personally—the priorities that govern us—are visible in our community witness. No one can legitimately claim the name of Jesus if he is known to be abusive or if he is a person with a bitter spirit. We must not be discourteous in our community. A real Christian goes the second and third mile and turns the other cheek.

Those are not easy things to do. You may suffer abuse when you turn the other cheek. You may be thought a fool when you "give your cloak also" (cf. Matt. 5:40). Jesus never said we would be appreciated if we obeyed Him. Being appreciated isn't a Christian priority; being careful not to cause anger and abuse by our ways and being an example of God's loving nature are Christian priorities. Christians help others. They care about the widows; they help the retired man who has a weak heart; they take extra time to sit on the porch and talk with neighbors. They won't fellowship only with other believers, feasting their souls in the pleasant company of like-minded people, while having nothing to do with those outside God who need life, love, and spiritual values.

Searching for Light

Christians should be careful to maintain secular relationships. We need to work at it and pray about it. Though we need time at home, how easy it is to carry that too far and always stay home and never attend a local political or town meeting. How nice to read a good book on faith rather than be a part of the school curriculum planning committee. But how critically important it is for us to leave our comforts and go out into the world with God. God keeps us in the world where we can be the salt of His presence to flavor and to preserve what would otherwise be tasteless or would rot without the influence of salt. Jesus said, "Ye are the salt of the earth" (Matt. 5:13). That's what we are! One way we can be salt where salt is needed is to make community involvement a priority in our lives.

We need to be careful not to be absorbed into the priorities of the world. We read in Scripture that all things were created by God and that they were created for our use. Paul said that nothing is unclean in itself (cf. Rom. 14:14). But recently there has been much grasping "gluttony" on the part of many Christians: gluttony for things, gluttony for pleasure, and gluttony of self-indulgence, to the point where self-indulgence has almost become a "Christian virtue"—a goal. Some Christians have become takers of things and users of people, and are no longer respected. In the darkness of a world searching for light, many Christians are not clear, illuminating lights. Jesus said, "Ye are the light of the world. A city that is set on a hill cannot be hid" (Matt. 5:14).

We are free in Christ, that is true. But when we come to the point of making a god of self, it is obvious to the community that our God doesn't really satisfy us. They then come to despise us for our duplicity. Whether or not the community has made gods for itself is not the issue. Non-Christians have nothing but the gods they make, grasp, and cling to. But we have the one true God. We lose that distinction when we run after pagan gods too.

One of the opportunities given to Christians today is to help their communities and the peoples of the world through giving. We can give our time and our money. Many people don't know how to give because they have neither the calling of God to do so nor the awareness of the needs of others.

We who belong to the One who came into the world—emptying Himself and giving Himself for us (Phil. 2:7-8)—can become givers too, for we have a new nature, the nature of Christ who "liveth in me" (Gal. 2:20).

We need to be aware of the spiritual as well as the physical situation of our fellow world dwellers. We need to know about people in our community who do not love Christ. Our time, our witness, our funds can help them. We can reach out daily in little ways: sending a smile to a lonely man, shoveling snow for a neighbor, giving an elderly friend a ride, cooking dinner for a sick neighbor, taking a youngster to Little League games, repairing a bike. And we can reach out in larger ways too, through missions or by caring for foster children.

Depth to Our Lives
Giving is an honor. Our Lord made it clear that "inasmuch as ye have done it unto one of the least of these My brethren, ye have done it unto Me" (Matt. 25:40). Those who give the least have the least left over. In fact, those who give the least are usually the biggest takers, no matter how rich they are. The Bible doesn't promise riches to those who give—ours isn't a "good deals" God. But He does care for us. He promised, "Give, and it shall be given unto you; good measure, pressed down, and shaken together, and running over, shall men give into your bosom. For with the same measure that ye mete withal it shall be measured to you again" (Luke 6:38). What He gives can't be bought—He gives Himself.

Day by day, giving adds depth to our lives. We grow by giving and others are blessed by it. Then they too become givers. One day my wife, Andrea, and I helped a young couple in need. They thanked us and said the usual about "never being able to repay you." We told them that years before others had helped us and someday they too would have the privilege of helping someone else. And they will! They will remember that someone gave to them, and they will give to others. That's the way it is when people are operating by God's rule and love. The blessings go on.

We have so much to give to our world; there is so much need. We can't touch all of it or even a small fraction of it, but we can reach out to someone in some way. We can do that today—right now. Are you ready to do it? Are you asking yourself how you can help others? Are you asking others how you can help them? Are you asking God?

Our actions in our communities, in our world, depend on the behavior established within ourselves, behavior patterns built on the practice of set priorities. We say, "This I will do," and we mean it as a vow before God. Our priorities make our freedom possible, which in turn makes our giving possible. Why? Because we are no longer "situational," we will give; we will help. It is not an issue to be debated afresh in each new situation.

Your being, your nature, your character are governed by the control on your life—and for the Christian, Jesus Christ is that control. That is a certainty for all who claim His ownership. As you go out into your world, you go not alone but with Him who controls you, whose life you have in you.

God's People Are Everywhere

The older I get the more I appreciate the Christian community. God has His people everywhere. One summer day, while my wife and I were driving to a hospital to visit a patient, the engine of our car blew out. We started walking, making our way to the home of a Christian friend who lived about a mile and a half away. We arrived hot and tired. The woman gave us a cold drink and then gave us her car keys so that we could drive home. I thought as we were driving home, "Isn't this wonderful! The Christian family is such that you can walk up to a house, ring the doorbell, be invited in, be given a cold drink, and then be loaned a car to drive home. Christians care about each other."

We can easily criticize the shortcomings of the Christian family (and there are many), but they are God's people and they are a community.

I used to think that there were very few believers in the world. I no longer think that way. I used to have a narrow view of the church, but no longer. There are believers everywhere who really care about others because they truly care about God. They see people for what they are, God's highest creation—"the world" for which Christ died (John 3:16). God's people are everywhere.

One day a woman telephoned our home. We did not know her and she did not know us. But she was a Christian, and she and others from her church had made a call on one of our elderly relatives. These Christians weren't from our church. They weren't even from our denomination, but they love the Lord Jesus. This woman and her friends ministered to our relative in ways that we could not because they were strangers. They were obeying Jesus—they were visiting the sick, and they helped our relative who had a need. We thanked her, told her that we too were believers, and explained that her witness to our relative was deeply appreciated.

That's Christian community! That's love! That's caring!

These are quiet Christians—not noisy ones—and they are all around. They care for others, not for money or praise but because there is a need. Responsibility for others is a priority for them. How different from those who seek acclaim and prestige, wanting to be noticed for their "work for God," while others quietly do most of the work for which they take credit. There have always been people like Ananias and Sapphira, people who want to be known as givers and doers but who give and do little. Jesus said of them, "They have their reward" (Matt. 6:16).

True Christian community is not flashy; it is obedience in practice. Down through the ages Christians have always given priority to

the apostles' doctrine and fellowship, and in breaking of bread, and in prayers. ... And all that believed were together, and had all things common; and sold their possessions and goods, and parted them to all men, as every man had need. And they, continuing daily with one accord in the temple, and breaking bread from house to house, did eat their meat with gladness and singleness of heart, praising God, and having favor with all the people (Acts 2:42, 44-47).

Christians in community are Christians who encourage, help, and build up one another. Barnabas was like that. Even his name describes encouragement (Acts 4:36). He was a great man who had obviously found peace with himself. He recognized who he was, his gifts, what he could do, what he could not do, and he lived out his priority before God as an encourager. He was pleased to build up others.

How sadly different from Barnabas are those who boast but do not know Christ or the value we have in Christ. They are so unsure of themselves and so insecure that the only way they can exist is by putting others down. They are advertising loud and clear how insecure, weak, and confused they are. They need to be important but they don't know how. They are trying to be "something" in their own eyes by making others appear to be lesser beings. That's a sickness in the world, a plague that tries to invade the body of believers. Sometimes it succeeds.

I can still feel the pain I felt in graduate school during sessions with my major advisor who claimed to be a Christian. Often entire conference sessions were spent in his ridiculing and criticizing me as a person. I remember coming home and saying to my wife, "I still don't know what is wrong with my thesis; all I know is what is wrong with me."

That professor had a need to put students down, never having outgrown the punishment he took at the hand of a professor who once did the same to him.

Putdowns, ridicule are a common story in the world. People who have opportunities to help, often hurt instead. As children they probably pulled wings off flies or pinched babies when no one was looking. Knowing that they were not strong in themselves, they had to prove to themselves that they could dominate others.

Christians secure in Christ will not behave that way. They belong to God. They are God's children. "But as many as received Him, to them gave He power to become the sons of God, even to them that believe on His name" (John 1:12). Christians are strong. Paul said, "I can do all things through Christ which strengtheneth me" (Phil. 4:13). Secure and strong, Christians don't need what insecure, weak people need. Christians want to be like their Master.

We Are Observed

No matter where we are, we live out our Christianity before others. One afternoon, during a three-week stay in Nairobi, Kenya, I went shopping in the native markets. I found a picture made out of banana tree bark, and I liked it. It would go nicely on a particular wall at home. So I asked the price and began to barter as the custom is there. But then what I was doing struck me. I was trying to barter about a price that, at current exchange rates, was only 17¢. There I stood, a rich American, trying to get a price down from 17¢ to 16¢, when the man who made the picture was selling it to earn his living. How could I justify giving money to international programs to feed people and then turn around and, for the sake of a penny, try to pay less to a man who was earning his living through his trade?

How are you treating the people around you? Are you a

giver or a taker? Are you a manipulator, a user? It isn't difficult to find manipulators. They are everywhere. I am sometimes frustrated by Christians who have no qualms about asking for favors to be done for them because they are Christians. They will take from others so long as it advances them or gives them added income or some free samples or gifts or discounts. They use people for personal gain. Jesus never did that.

People Know What We Are Like
Our priorities show. People know what we are like. We can't disguise that. One day I was standing in the cashier's line at the New Otani Hotel in Tokyo. A woman approached the desk and asked for the free postcards that the hotel gives to guests. The young man behind the desk was polite and asked how many she would like to have. "Several," she replied. He looked puzzled. "How many?" he asked.

"I said several," she snarled. She knew that he didn't understand and she enjoyed his squirming. There was silence as she looked at him defiantly, letting him know that she thought he was pretty stupid. He struggled for a minute and then said, "Seven?"

"I said several," she repeated. And, still confused by the word "several," he counted out seven cards and gave them to her with a smile. As she walked away she shouted out a phrase in French. She was letting him know that she knew a foreign language. Never mind that it was French and she was in Japan. Never mind that she didn't know Japanese but expected him to know her English slang. Never mind that she was well aware that he didn't understand her word; she wasn't going to choose a word that he did know. She left that poor young man embarrassed and hurt.

Day by day, pray for those you will meet, especially considering your interactions with them. One word, one action, like a Hebrew blessing, has a life of its own and cannot be quickly recalled. It is alive, for once in someone's mind, it stays there. Are you praying about your priorities in the community, in the world?

The Bible says, "Be not deceived; God is not mocked; for whatsoever a man soweth, that shall he also reap" (Gal. 6:7). There is something miraculous about a harvest. The harvest is greater than the number of seeds planted. When a farmer plants, he expects a harvest for his table, a harvest to sell, and enough left over for the next year's planting. Similarly, what you do that is destructive and sinful will spread and grow like seeds planted and will bring a harvest of destructive weeds that will choke out everything—your spirit and soul, those in your immediate community, those in the larger community—everything you touch.

But if you sow constructive seeds which pertain to life, they will grow and multiply; the harvest will be so great that everyone will benefit, and there will be more seeds for planting.

Learn to submit your life to the wishes of the One who came not to be served but to serve. Learn to control your desires, and learn to think of others, not to be a taker—that is maturity. That's why the Christian community can be, and often is, far more mature than the hedonistic culture surrounding it. Christians have come to terms with reality, learning who they are, recognizing the resources of their lives and the wealth available from Him who owns "the cattle upon a thousand hills" (Ps. 50:10). Christians with true priorities are able to obey the Scripture which encourages: "Finally, brethren, whatsoever things are true, whatsoever things are honest, whatsoever things are just, whatsoever things are pure, whatsoever things are lovely, whatsoever things are of good report; if there be any virtue, and if there be any praise, think on these things" (Phil. 4:8).

Christians learn to think on those things and such things permeate their lives. The world is richer because they do.

Whose Work Are You Doing? On Whose Time?

10

We work for money. Yet money has no value in itself. Its value is only in what it can buy. It is not an end, a complete satisfaction of our work. The real satisfaction in work is the accomplishment of a job well done. If our only satisfaction is a larger paycheck, we have gained little. More money can buy a temporary escape, a few pleasures, but they are quickly past. Work as an achievement is the more satisfying reward.

In 1961, after seven years of university and seminary education in which I had to work two, and sometimes three, part-time jobs to pay my way, I was ordained to the ministry at a salary of $4,000 a year.

I knew that others with the same number of years in university and graduate school were earning much larger salaries, but none that I knew enjoyed the rewards that I was experiencing. I was caring for the spiritual needs of a congregation. Had money been a goal, I would have been miserable because I was earning hardly enough to scrape by.

Why do you work? What do you work for? It would be a terrible thing if at retirement, after a lifetime of working, you could only say of those years spent working, "I earned money."

119

Seeing the Accomplishment

Properly disciplined, any person can accomplish great work. But he must learn to redeem the time. Most of us don't realize it, and certainly our culture with its emphasis on pleasure and ease doesn't encourage it, but we have more energy and time for work than we think. One of the great satisfactions in life is seeing the accomplishments brought by hard work. Yet many of us have lost our sense of value because we have not had that sense of accomplishment. We have not had difficult hard work and the satisfaction of mastering it.

We can do far more than we think we can, but we need to measure the results. We need to know how to keep our goals before us so that we can see the accomplishments of some small projects as steps toward our goals.

One spring I had been working without weekend breaks for five weeks and faced three more such weeks. In the midst of other travels, I spent a week at the Evangelical Press Association meetings which ended on a Wednesday evening. By Thursday morning most of the EPA people had gone. My own production editor, who also had attended that meeting, caught an early morning flight and went directly to the office to take care of the work there. We had an understanding that if anything had to have my attention, it could be brought to my home that evening so that it would be ready the next morning. With those arrangements, I scheduled a late afternoon flight. That left me the entire morning and early afternoon to work.

I checked out of my room, left my baggage with a porter, and found a quiet corner in the hotel lobby. There I sat down at a table and spread out all the work that I had not been able to get to during the past weeks of travel. It was a quiet time— no telephone, nobody pushing for answers—and I was able to work, sit back and think, take notes, and go over my priorities. It was one of the most productive periods of time that I had had in weeks.

I could have rushed back to the office, but it cost no more to stay those extra hours, and I knew they would be quiet hours—a time to reflect, a time to think.

We all need those times to think. Whether we are writers or window washers, engineers or electricians, there is no reason why occasionally some such retreat can't be found to help put thoughts, plans, and work into the order of our priorities.

You can go to a park with a note pad and think. You can sit on the grass or on a bench in a cemetery. You can go to a library. You can spend an hour in an old downtown hotel with a large sitting area. A local college campus has lots of niches where you can be quiet. Whatever you do, there is value in occasionally making a priority of checking your priorities. In the long run these mini-breaks save time and frustration.

I fly a great deal and often look for out-of-the-way places in an airport where I can work. For example, some airline waiting areas are vacant between flights, especially those of small airlines. I find them and read, take notes, or work on manuscripts. Late evenings and nights at airports are especially quiet.

Why take work home at night if that's a "tired time" for you? On the other hand, if you are a night person, use those times when the pressure is off and the time is there at the end of the day; it can be productive. You may work better in early morning when the house is still quiet. But to do that, you can't stay up late at night. Find your best time and use it. Why? Because it ought to be a priority of your life to use time wisely.

God has given each of us a certain number of days to live on this earth. Without pressure or panic we can make each of those days worthwhile. Someday, because we took time before God to evaluate our priorities and to plan the steps necessary for fulfilling them, we will be able to say, "Master, You gave me ten talents and here are ten more."

Long walks are productive for thinking, and they are good exercise too. I can dictate ideas, notes, or letters on a recorder while I am walking.

For example, I had a meeting coming up for which I needed to get a lot of questions answered. Walking time was a good time to think through the questions and dictate answers. When I had the list typed, I was prepared for the meeting. It saved my time and the time of the other people at the meeting because I knew exactly what information I needed and could go down the list. And I got good exercise while making that list.

Renewal Time

Most executives know that travel isn't romantic; it's time consuming, tiring. There are the long hours on a plane, not sleeping well in a hotel, not feeling sharp the next day, the need to telephone the office for notes that you wish you had brought along but that subject wasn't supposed to be on the agenda . . . and so it goes. People are much more efficient in familiar settings. I would rather use the phone than travel; it's cheaper and I get more done by not traveling. If I must travel, I would rather do it in blocks of time so that I have similar blocks of time at the office, rather than always being about to go or come—which is disruptive, tiring, and hinders fulfilling my job goals.

At home, with work waiting to think about, or a Sunday School lesson to prepare, I allow my mind to lie fallow while I am polishing my shoes. Then my mind can go back to work on the difficult tasks knowing that I will "reward" myself a half hour or an hour later with another fallow time doing some other mundane chore.

I have a basement remodeling project that is on-going. Working on it is a restful time that renews me for the mental work of writing. Family time can be scheduled too, so that it is not time taken away from a work project but is a rewarding renewal time. Family time actually helps me be a happier person which influences my work. This doesn't put less value on family time, but more. Family time is special; it is set-aside time. Redeeming the time means that time given to not working can be as much quality time as that given to working.

There is great joy in redeeming the time. Busy people can actually have more time for their families than those who are not so busy. Certainly they have more time than lazy people, because lazy people tend to grind along, accomplishing little, with small tasks filling large time spaces. If a person doesn't know how to work, he probably won't know how to truly rest either. He is always doing the same things. He doesn't know the joy of total concentration on one project in order to have total concentration on another project, or to have nonconcentration by design—enjoying play and laughter simply for the sake of playing and laughing. Time usage is an important priority in a disciplined Christian's life.

In Scripture, the ant is used as an example of a hard worker. "Consider her ways, and be wise; which having no guide, overseer, or ruler, provideth her meat in the summer, and gathereth her food in the harvest" (Prov. 6:6-8). The lazy man is said to be more interested in "a little sleep, a little slumber, a little folding of the hands to sleep" (Prov. 6:10). So not wanting to be like the lazy man, we think we should keep going; we want to be like the ant. Yet Jesus could say, "Come ye yourselves apart . . . and rest a while" (Mark 6:31).

In the balance between work and rest, we use our time for what it is, God's gift to us. The gift is to be redeemed—mentally, physically, emotionally, and spiritually. Redeeming the time is part of honoring God. He knows our days; He knows our time; He knows our families; He knows our work projects; He knows what we are doing with them. He also knows what we are not doing with them.

God Expects Us to Work

We do not live in the Garden of Eden. Adam and Eve could have been put to death after the Fall, but they were allowed to work. That is God's provision. "That every man may eat and drink, and find satisfaction in all his toil—this is the gift of God" (Ecc. 3:13, NIV).

Paul warned, "For even when we were with you, this we commanded you, that if any would not work, neither should he eat" (2 Thes. 3:10). He also condemned busybodies who gossip rather than work.

God expects us to work. Work is as much an act of worship as any other part of the presentation of ourselves to God called for in Romans 12:1-2. That's why we are not to cheat on the job or waste time.

Don't be an average worker. Being above average is difficult in any place of business because there are usually clock watchers who will criticize you for your hard work. Some fellow employees will always try to get by with as little work as possible, and they resent anyone who doesn't do as they do. But you don't have to be an average worker. You are gifted by God. Exercise those gifts, and you will find the reward of work satisfaction that so many people miss. Very few people have ever given their total energy to their work. Those who do are the accomplishing ones.

There is a time and place for rest, but work time isn't one of them. We owe 100 percent of our work efforts to our employer as responsible workers. God didn't put us on this earth to waste time, energy, or to steal from the people who employ us—even to witness to the faith!

A friend told me about his experience with a zealous Christian. At work the Christian brother came to him and asked, "Are you saved?"

My friend replied, "Yes, I am."

"How do you know that you're saved?"

"Because I believe John 3:16 and I have committed my life to Jesus Christ. And, because I am a Christian, I don't believe in stealing; so, since we are both on company time, let's get back to work."

We will have opportunities to share our faith, but we only have the right to do it on our own time. We are to be faithful, hardworking employees on our employer's time. A Christian doesn't worship his job. He worships God. But because he worships God, he does good work—the two go together.

Your Contribution to the World

Another point to consider in your work is your contribution to the world. We remember great preachers, writers, artists, educators, and inventors because they influence our lives. William Shakespeare has influenced our lives; so have Booker T. Washington, Augustine, Rembrandt, and Beethoven. But who remembers those who only labored for money—or, if they are remembered, who can say, "They helped me"?

In the final analysis, no one will remember your salary level, but many will remember and call you blessed if, as you earned a living, you were faithful and put your greatest energies into what lasts. The way to do that is to "do all to the glory of God" (1 Cor. 10:31). That kind of life will show, it will influence, and it will bless. No matter whether you work with a shovel, a typewriter, or a computer, your work reflects your view of God, and others will detect that view. Therefore, work well. Let your work say, "I work for a higher purpose. I work for God." People will notice, and there may be many with you in heaven who will say, "I'm here because I worked beside you. I saw the difference in your life."

God Brings Out the Best

Who is your boss? Some people have never established who or what governs them. We are not to be governed by a paycheck but by God. When we work with, not against, God's control, we move into a smooth relationship. God brings out the best of our skills, our mind, our time, our preferences, our experiences, and our training. He is always with us when we are open to His best in our working lives. God's way is always the best for us because God is not the God of confusion (see 1 Cor. 14:33).

Knowing who is "boss" is freeing. The One who made us is the One who controls. He knows us, and He knows what gifts He gave to us. He knows what we can do.

Unfortunately, a widespread feeling prevails that somehow somebody owes me something. The government owes me something; the state owes me something; industry owes me something; my parents owe me something. People who adopt that attitude are always trapped. They are governed by the feeling of being cheated and manipulated. Whether subtly or overtly, they hit back.

Supervisors taking management training courses are told that they can often determine a person's work habits by the era in which that person grew up. That came to mind one day when I was a guest lecturer in a journalism class at a local college. Before the class began I was talking with the teacher about job opportunities for students. She said, "I hope you will tell them that they have got to have some performance to show. They don't believe me; I can't even get them to be concerned about proper grammar and spelling in their letters of application. They think that a company should hire them because of who they are."

She told me that a young man recently told her that he would go get a job with *Decision* magazine.

"And what do you have to offer *Decision*?" the teacher asked.

"What do you mean 'offer'?"

"Well, what skills do you have? What experience? What makes you a candidate for a position?"

The student was bewildered. He thought that his personality would get him a job.

Two days later I picked up a newspaper and read a column written by a 17-year-old high school student in which she was stating why, in her opinion, an employer should hire her. Her first and primary reason was, "Because I feel good about myself." She listed a few other qualifications such as "I love to meet new people" / "I have experienced working and enjoy it" (not that she has had significant work experience but that she has experienced working and enjoys it). And her summary was, "In conclusion, I think an employer should hire me because I'm me and that's the most that I'll ever be."

I receive one or two letters a week from people who want jobs. They have been taught by resumé writers that they should sell themselves by talking about their good points. And so they come on strong with huge egos. There are no problems in our office that they cannot handle, they inform me. They can completely streamline our organization, eliminate waste, and build a strong staff. But some of them don't even know how to spell the name of our magazine, nor have they had any writing experience.

Just the other day I met a young man who said, "I want to be a manager."

"What would you like to manage?" I asked.

"Anything. I can manage anything."

"How much experience have you had?" He didn't have any. "Education?" He had finished high school. But he could manage any business; he knew that he could.

If a person feels called to a job, then certainly he is also called to train for that job. If he will not work hard to get the required education for that job, why should anyone believe that he will work hard later?

I have had college graduates work for me who have not even known basic office procedures. They didn't know that they couldn't read the newspaper for half an hour in the middle of the day. They didn't know that they couldn't spend an hour writing letters to their friends on company time. They didn't know that they couldn't leave the office and go for a walk downtown because "it's warm and the sun is shining." I've seen all these things happen, and when I have spoken to them about their nonwork activities, they haven't been able to grasp what I was talking about. "Why not?" they have asked.

The Joy of Sore Muscles

Some people scoff at the old Puritan work ethic, but it is time to dust it off—to know the joy of sore muscles from hard work, to have a sense of accomplishment at the end of a day, to know that you have done your best, to know the joy of good sleep because of hard work done, and to know that a paycheck is earned—that it is not a gift.

Our work is our ministry, and we do it for the Lord. Work should be satisfying; we spend the better part of the day for most of our lives working. But work isn't an end in itself. We ought to be satisfied with what we do before the Lord—and offer it to Him.

It doesn't matter what kind of work we do, or what kind of title is on our door; as Christians we serve the Lord. That means we work toward competency, faithfulness, and honesty. God will use our faithfulness on any job if our work is done for Him.

When I was a student at Wayne State University in Detroit, I worked one summer remodeling a bookstore. It was hot, dirty work. Often the humidity was so high that sweat just rolled off the workers. One particularly hot day, when we were working in the back room, the boss said that someone had to clean the furnace ducts. I volunteered to do it. Anyone who has ever cleaned furnace ducts on a hot, humid day knows what it was like, but it was the job I had to do and any job can be done for the Lord. As I worked, I found myself whistling. In a few minutes someone who was cleaning shelves on the other side of the room yelled over, "What are you whistling?" I hadn't consciously realized that I had been whistling a Gospel song until he asked. So I told him and gave him the words of the song. He didn't respond. But, unknown to both of us, another worker was behind some other bookshelves and he had heard both the whistling and our conversation. He asked a question that later opened the door to conversation about the saving work of Jesus Christ. I didn't know it when I was working; I didn't know it when I was whistling; I didn't know it when I was speaking to the first man, but God was preparing that second man to hear the Gospel message. We are to work and be faithful—that's a priority. Sometimes God uses our work for something extra, even when the perspiration is streaming down our backs and the soot is in our eyes.

What We Can't Do

How are you spending your time? What is important to you? What is your priority about work? You need to know the answers for quite another reason than just to apply your gifts to accomplishments. You need to know so that you can recognize what your gifts are and what they are not, so that you don't try to do what somebody else can do better.

For years I spun my wheels on administrative details. I wanted to plan things and develop ideas, but answering letters, filing, and other detail work got in the way, and I hated it. I'd end up shoving lots of bits and pieces of paper around my desk without accomplishing much of the work I wanted to do. One day when I was a campus minister, a woman in our church came to me and said, "You need to be organized, and I'm going to do it." She worked three days a week handling administrative details for me. A year later my wife commented, "Your production has increased threefold since you got her help." She was right. Since that time, with the help of capable people who like to do what I don't like to do and thus do it infinitely better, my work has improved.

I used to hesitate giving people certain jobs because I didn't like doing those jobs myself. I assumed that everyone was like me. Foolish? Yes, it was, but I had to learn. I had to learn that what I can't do, others can do very well. I had to learn that they like to do some of the things that I don't like to do. I help them and they help me, if we all know our particular gifts. On the *Decision* magazine staff, we have people who are much better at certain jobs than I am. That makes good use of my time and good use of their talents.

Learn to work with your abilities. Learn to get the help of others when you can. You will work better, and that's always a high priority for a Christian.

Seek advice about your work; get it whenever you can. Don't be so proud that you can't learn from someone else. I've met shop foremen who wouldn't listen to their subordinates. They thought it somehow lessened them and their positions. Instead of taking the opportunity to strengthen their abilities through counsel, they refused to admit that anyone could tell them anything. They wouldn't learn because they thought there wasn't anything they didn't know. The Bible says, "Where no counsel is, the people fall, but in the multitude of counselors there is safety" (Prov. 11:14). Those who are serious about serving God will take counsel. God teaches us through others.

You only have one life; live it well by working well. I know a man who sets an example that any Christian can follow. He picks up the garbage in front of our house. When he stops his truck and jumps out, he is on a dead run. With fluid motions the garbage cans are emptied, and he is back in his truck, moving down the street. Yet he is always kind. If someone is on vacation, or if there is an elderly person in the house, he puts his large container on his shoulder, goes to the back of the house and dumps their garbage into his portable container, and carries the garbage out to the front. He doesn't charge extra for that, but makes it a part of his work. And if someone wants to talk, he'll take a minute to chat, but then he is running again.

He is a man who knows how to use his energy without wasting any of it. He knows how to give good service beyond what is expected.

Can a Christian who is called by the name that is higher than any other name do any less in the vocation to which he is called? May it always be said of every Christian, "He knows how to work."

Worship, a High View of God

11

Sooner or later we come to a point in our lives where we stop asking for new and exciting devotional helps, the latest teaching on prayer, messages on quiet time, and get about the business of worshiping God. Too many Christians want a quick spiritual fix. They want to know how they can lift their low spirits or how they can enjoy the Lord. They want to read about actors, sports figures, and wealthy business people who are "spiritually successful." But God wants people who are more interested in meeting with Him than in just reading about other people who meet with Him. If you want to read about someone who truly worshiped God, read about Jesus in the Gospels. Jesus loved the Father. His priority was to worship and serve. "I seek not Mine own will, but the will of the Father which hath sent Me" (John 5:30). He would get up a great while before day and go off alone to pray. Was He ever tired? Did He ever want to "skip it"? Follow His schedule in Mark 3—5. He was so pressed that He couldn't even eat (3:20) and throngs pushed in about Him (5:24). He was just like us, tempted as we are. But His meeting with the Father was so critically important to Him that it was a driving priority. He wanted time for worship so He made time for it (Matt. 14:23; Luke 6:12).

Our First and Greatest Priority

The desire to worship is a desire to be with God—to hear Him, to enjoy Him, to honor Him, and to praise Him. You know whether or not you want to do that. If you don't want to worship God, you won't, no matter how many books you read about it.

Too many people don't worship; instead they just attend worship services. They love God superficially for the same reason they love another person: for what that person "does for me." They don't want to worship God; they want to receive a glow, a warmth, an answer to prayer, a reward of some kind.

To worship, we need to do what the old Quakers called "centering down," applying ourselves to what God is saying, focusing on who God is and on what He is doing, and applying it to our lives because God wants us to.

We won't spend much time with God if we are concentrating only on ourselves; we will think only in terms of our schedule, our program, our ministry, and not in terms of God. We will measure prayer by the accomplishments wrought through prayer and not by the relationship that comes from being with God.

When do you pray? Do you have a set time for prayer? If you don't, you are probably wasting huge amounts of your time. In prayer we wait for God's instruction. Because of prayer we won't rush ahead of God in spiritual arrogance, as James warned, saying, "Today or tomorrow we will" (see James 4:13 ff). In prayer we recognize that our first and greatest priority in life is to know God and to love Him with all our heart, soul, mind, and strength.

I have pondered why I like staying home so much, because friends often tell me, "I wish I could travel as you do." I've come to realize that a lot of my wanting to stay home is built around my quiet time with God. It is regular, it is systematic, it is disciplined—it gives me steady growth and regular worship. I need that.

When travel enters in, especially overseas travel with time changes and different environments, as well as different schedules that are controlled by others, everything gets off balance. The discipline of my daily worship time with God becomes irregular, and I miss it. Travel hurts me in many ways spiritually because I am a person who likes a system. I need it for spiritual growth.

An Encounter with God

Worship is a priority for me. Worship doesn't only mean going to church. Going to church may include worship, but I have been blocked from worship in church too. Emphases on "performances" have taken my eyes away from God. Following a printed program, listening to a sermon, hearing a choir—all these may aid in worship, but only if I have a personal encounter with God. Worship in church is a climax, a time with other believers who also have had an ongoing worship all week long. Paul said, "I beseech you therefore, brethren, by the mercies of God, that ye present your bodies a living sacrifice, holy, acceptable unto God, which is your reasonable service. And be not conformed to this world; but be ye transformed by the renewing of your mind, that ye may prove what is that good, and acceptable, and perfect will of God" (Rom. 12:1-2).

That presentation of ourselves is worship. As I do that daily, and as others do that daily, then our coming together on Sunday is the result of a week of "presentation." We look forward to an encounter with God that is precious and corporate because it comes out of our fullness, not out of our emptiness. It comes not because we haven't met God all week but because we have. When we come to a worship service full of adoration and praise, then the music, the Bible exposition, the praying, and the Scripture blesses us as we corporately enter into a presentation of ourselves to God as a culmination of all our individual "presentings." But without presenting ourselves as "living sacrifices," there will not be true worship—only the observation of performance. The priority of a believer is to "seek His face." The psalmist said, "I, O Lord, cry to Thee; in the morning my prayer comes before Thee" (Ps. 88:13, RSV). And that is every day.

Why We Need Worship

In worship we are able to balance the tension between fear and grace. God is totally omnipotent. He is the God "out there." There is no human reason why He should have any concern for us. The psalmist wrote: "What is man, that Thou art mindful of him?" (Ps. 8:4) People fear God, which is sensible and reasonable when we recognize who He is—His purity, His omniscience, His excellence, and His power. For He is the judging God. Yet, He is also the God of grace—the truly loving One who "so loved the world, that He gave His only begotten Son" (John 3:16). He is the One who comes seeking and pleading for our return to Him. He is the One who in Christ Jesus came "to seek and to save that which was lost" (Luke 19:10).

Throughout the Scriptures the thread of God's seeking love is woven. We misunderstand God if we are only frightened of Him. But we misunderstand as well if, because of His compassion for us, we think we can be buddies with Him. We don't walk through life with an arm around the shoulder of God, as some Gospel songs imply. We are not equals with Him. That's why we need to worship Him.

In worship we grasp the tension between God who is both totally outside and beyond creation and yet who is closer than any friend can be. In worship we identify the miracle of seeking grace. We see the One who loves us, even though we see by His holiness how unholy we are.

When we think about who He is and what He has done for us, our worship becomes praise. In response to our praise comes yet a greater outpouring of His grace and love to which we then respond even more. So as God's children, we respectfully honor, worship, listen to, and adore Him. As we worship God in His holiness and splendor, He has opportunity to speak to us and to direct us as His children. In worship, we understand the dimensions of what He has done in seeking us through His great self-emptying (cf. Phil. 2). In worship we grasp something of the greatness of God A low view of God tends to decrease our view of His nearness and His leadership. Only a high view of the Deity allows us some grasp of the Incarnation and redemptive ministry of God and brings us to true worship.

Our priority is to learn more and more of Him. The more we learn, the more we will worship. The opposite is also true: the less we know of God, the less we will worship. The less we know of God, the more we will have an "anything-is-OK" view of worship. Sloppy worship shows a disrespect for God and keeps us from an understanding of life itself; for the One we worship is the One who created, owns, guides, and completes us.

Do We Need the Church?

"But," people ask, "can't I just love God on my own? Do I really need the church?" The answer is explained in Ephesians 4:11-16. We are to love the church. Jesus did; He gave Himself for the church (Eph. 5:25). That means we won't tear it down or criticize it. It is the body of Christ, the gathering of the committed, the believers; we need each other.

In fact, if we look at Scripture, it tells us to have peace with one another, love one another, prefer one another, and be of the same mind with one another. We are to edify one another, receive one another, admonish one another, greet one another, wait for one another, care for one another, and serve one another. We are not to consume, bite, or devour one another, envy one another, or judge one another. We are to bear one another's burdens, be kind to one another, and stir up one another to good works. We are not to speak evil of others or grumble against each other. We are to confess our faults to each other, pray for one another, practice hospitality with one another, and minister through our gifts to one another.

How are we going to do all that? We are going to do it by recognizing that Christ is the Lord of the church and that He is our Lord. Because we love our Lord and serve Him, we will love and serve the church.

He put you in your church with your skills and your talents for a purpose. That doesn't mean you're to do everything in the church, but you are to make the work of your church a priority. You are to be supportive with your finances, your time, your prayers, and your abilities.

Is giving money one of your worship priorities? Do you give as careful thought to your giving as businessmen do to their investments? In our house we give to our local church and to other ministries that we believe are showing faithfulness to Christ.

Are you supportive of church leaders? Do you pray for them? Do you pray for your pastor? I have been a pastor and I know how lonely that position can be. Pray for your pastor and his family; allow him time to be a person and time to be alone with his family.

I know a pastor who will work only 50 hours a week. He spends at least three nights a week at home with his family. When the elders ask him to do more calling, he asks, "What shall I cut out?" He has priorities. He says, "If I don't have priorities about my work, how can I make a statement to the workaholics in the congregation?"

Do the work of ministry, but do it as God gives you His gifts. Don't feel guilty if you're not the teacher. Don't feel guilty if your gift is hospitality and not administration or evangelism. You can't do it all. You're to be a witness, but that's not something you do so much as something you are. It happens by staying close to Christ.

Those who think they "do" witnessing are often the ones who get in the way so that people see them rather than Christ. An introducer is a person who introduces two people and then gets out of the way so they can become acquainted. If I introduce a young man to a young woman, do I stay and monopolize the conversation or do I get out of the way? Is "introducing" people to the Lord a priority in your life? Can you do it so that they are impressed with the Saviour and not with you and your skills as an introducer? Can you work without drawing attention to yourself?

People who are evangelists are convinced Christians. They believe that evangelism is important. They are listeners—compulsive talkers are not good evangelists because they end up talking about themselves more than about Jesus. Effective evangelism is four fifths listening and one fifth speaking. Evangelistic listeners are empathetic; they try to enter into the feelings of other people.

Evangelists are not necessarily eloquent or glib or ready with all the answers, but they do try to articulate the Gospel clearly. True evangelism means trusting God week after week after week even when no immediate results are seen.

Are there jobs in the church that you think are beneath your dignity? I know people who will lead a morning service but who will not pull weeds from the church yard. I know people who will serve on the board of deacons but who will not pray for weaker Christians without gossiping about them. We are to exercise our gifts. But service is a priority too, done under the authority of God and for His glory. That is also your "presentation," your proper worship.

Are You Abiding?

As you discover your spiritual gifts, and others in the church discover theirs, you'll begin to relax and realize, "I don't have to be out there evangelizing if that's not my gift. I am to be a witness, but I may not be an evangelist. I don't have to be organizing a church supper if that is not my gift. I don't have to teach a Sunday School class; there are others to whom God has given that gift."

A body has two eyes, two ears, one mouth, two feet; you don't have to be all of them in the body of Christ. A foot doesn't have to be an ear; it would do an awful job as an ear. Let God develop His body, the church, His way. Then the work will go on, with everybody exercising their gifts.

What do you tell a Christian who says he doesn't have a gift? While he may be hoping he won't have to do anything, you ought to help him discover his gift. In doing so, you will be helping him to worship. It's our responsibility as a body of believers to recognize each other's gifts. We will all be growing Christians if we know our gifts and use them. Then, those of us who say, "I believe," will know our priorities and serve Him obediently.

The word abide appears three times in John 15:4, the account of the Vine and the branches: "Abide in Me, and I in you. As the branch cannot bear fruit of itself, except it abide in the vine; no more can ye, except ye abide in Me." Are you attached to the Vine? Are you abiding, ready to bear the fruit that He produces because you are concentrating on abiding, not taking inventory of the fruit production?

God opposes the proud, but look what He gives to the

humble—His grace (James 4:6). "Humble yourselves therefore under the mighty hand of God, that He may exalt you in due time" (1 Peter 5:6). That is what worship is, a humbling of ourselves under the mighty hand of God in surrender, obedience, and commitment. Our worship is to humble ourselves, and from that worship comes God's grace, His favor. What more could any of us want? What else could any of us ever need?

Follow God carefully and prayerfully, and both you and your church will benefit. Bit by bit, each person will be growing in Him and serving Him in the areas where he or she is strongest. You will see gifts being used, you will relax more, you will love God more, and you will rejoice more. That's what God wants.

The Holy Spirit knows what He is doing. Let God do His work in His church through your surrender to Him. God does His work very well.

Don't Just Take Up Space

Look at your priorities: Does Christ own you so that you fit in the body? Are you committed to His church—the body—because you need to be and want to be? God put you here at this time and place to be His, in His church. Don't just take up space. Remember the statement about the unproductive tree (Luke 13:6-9). If you feel you cannot worship or that you have no gift, examine your heart. Are you sure you are His? Being certain of that is of first importance. Does Christ know you as His own? Have you transferred your faith from yourself to Christ? What are you waiting for? Don't be tossed around any more by every wind of doctrine (Eph. 4:14). He promised, "Him that cometh to Me I will in no wise cast out" (John 6:37). After you have settled your relationship and your priorities of worship, your service and discipleship will also begin to be established.

You are holy. God has made you so. Don't ever profane or cheapen God's holy work—yourself. Make sure, as a priority of your life, that you practice absolute obedience to God so that nothing about you or what you do ever detracts from His beauty, or hinders His message, or degrades the name you bear. It is your priority to worship so that "whatsoever ye do, do all to the glory of God" (1 Cor. 10:31). "Be ye doers of the Word, and not hearers only" (James 1:22).

Everything you do is measured by the priority of this question: "Is my life lived in the worship and honor of God?"

The Pleasure of a Satisfying Life

12

Over the years I have learned a lesson: God doesn't take wrong turns.

It was late in the evening and I was trying to study. I was a third-year student at Wayne State University and, though I was trying to fight it, I knew that God was calling me into the ministry.

I didn't want that, but I couldn't ignore Him. Finally, in anguish I slammed my books shut, looked toward heaven, and cried out miserably, "All right, if that's what You want, that's what I'll do—but whatever happens, it's all Your fault!"

I didn't know it then, but I was beginning a journey that would prove over and over again that in the economy of God nothing is ever wasted. I would come to learn that God has priorities, that He doesn't make mistakes, and that He is guiding our lives; God doesn't take wrong turns. And now when I meet people who have made some seemingly foolish turns in their lives or have spent years doing what appeared to them to be the wrong thing, I tell them that God knows exactly what He is doing. In a drifting world, if He knows that our priority is to obey Him and follow Him, then, no matter how things seem, God has a purpose for us, a direction. He wastes nothing. I know that now, having learned it from what I thought were my own "wrong turns."

My first "wrong turn" came while I was still in theological seminary. I was convinced, because of some success in working with young people during my college days, that God wanted me in the military chaplaincy. Where else, I thought, would I find so many young people who needed spiritual help? So, as I moved along in my theological studies, I had my life's work all planned out. But when I graduated from seminary and applied for the chaplaincy, I was told to take a pastorate, get some experience, and then apply for the chaplaincy in a couple of years.

One evening, while visiting with a physician in the little town in West Virginia where I served as a pastor, I said, "You know, I pay a little extra on my insurance premium because I was once told I had a heart murmur. I don't think I have a heart murmur; why don't you check me so that I can get rid of that extra cost." So he did.

"I can't tell you that you don't have it," he said, "because you do."

"Well, how bad is it?" I asked.

He replied, "Oh, it's no problem; there are no restrictions on what you can do." Then he paused and added, "Oh, they'd never take you into military service."

My heart sank. All that preparation and planning wasted. All those years in school. What was God doing to me?

I Didn't Tell You That

Yet during that time our ministry to high school students in that little town was growing so fast that it was spreading across denominational lines and reaching large numbers of kids. As that work kept expanding, it was as if God said—and

I at last heard Him—"Look, I want you to work with young people. You're the one who decided that it had to be in the military chaplaincy. I didn't tell you that."

Today, across the country there are people in the ministry who were called of God through the work that He gave me in that little West Virginia town. And years afterward, when I was too old for military service, doctors told me that my heart murmur had completely disappeared.

In 1964, I was called to a pastorate in New Jersey and began the steps toward another "wrong turn." The New Jersey church was close to Rutgers University and, after a short time, students in sizable numbers began attending the church. Since my predecessor had been studying at Princeton Seminary while he pastored the church, and since the church's official board encouraged this, I started a graduate program in counseling at Princeton.

The ministry among students continued to grow and soon I began to worry that I was slighting the regular parishioners in favor of the students. I felt a tension building within me because I was taking time from the ongoing ministry with the established congregation to work with the students.

Then, midway through my graduate program at Princeton, I was invited to become a campus minister at Michigan State University. Everything seemed to be fitting into place. Not only would I be working full-time with students, but Michigan State was one of two universities in the country that offered a graduate program in counseling for pastors and that accepted credits from Princeton Seminary. Rejoicing that all things were working together for good, I resigned from the church, packed my household goods, and moved my family to Michigan. A few days after I arrived, Michigan State canceled that particular graduate program in counseling.

There I was with half the work completed toward a degree and no way to finish it. God had made a mistake, or so it seemed to me.

He Still Wasn't Finished

Yet during that year I found that what I needed for ministry with the students was exactly the kind of training that I'd received during my time at Princeton. Through individual counseling and group sessions during six school years, many students put their lives together by placing their faith in Jesus Christ. Through the traumatic days of campus unrest, these students hammered out a tough faith and found in Christ the answers to the questions they struggled with in their hearts.

A number of pastors and trained church leaders came out of the ministry at MSU during those eventful days. Though I never completed the full program at Princeton, God had given me precisely the training I needed for that student work. He hadn't made a mistake at all. He knew ahead of time what would be required to reach the searching men and women on campuses during those times. And He still wasn't finished with my "wrong turns."

The board of directors of that student ministry encouraged me to continue on with graduate studies because it would stretch me and it would be good for my students to see that I was in school with them. But what would I study?

One day during a visit with my sister, she said, "You always liked to write; why don't you study journalism?" At first it struck me as an odd idea, but the thought wouldn't go away. It seemed right, and nothing else gave me quite the same sense of leading.

So I enrolled in Michigan State's School of Communication Arts at the graduate level, majoring in journalism. Yet even as I explained to people what I was doing it really didn't make much sense to me. My seminary studies had been in Bible and theology, my graduate work in counseling; now here I was in seminars with publishers and editors, studying the management and operation of newspapers and magazines, law, and the history of the press, as well as other subjects pertaining to the print medium in our society.

But I stayed in the program, and when I graduated with my Master of Arts degree, my denomination requested a book on the Jesus movement (*The Jesus Kids*) because none of their established writers had enough experience with young people to capture the then "phenomenon" of street people turning to Jesus Christ. That book was scarcely finished when another (*The Christian and the Occult*) was in the works, because in my travels researching the first book I found so much material for the second.

Then other invitations began to come to write for magazines, and I was busy writing whenever I wasn't with students. God knew what He was doing as He prepared me to write.

The Next Phrase

But God had yet another step planned. My "wrong turn" in moving to Michigan State and enrolling in journalism because the counseling program wasn't available, combined with my earlier seminary work, was what God used to take me into the next phase of my life.

By 1972 the campus was beginning to quiet down. Vietnam demonstrations were in the past. Some educators even spoke about a return to the attitudes of the 1950s. Campus ministry was shaping up to be a training time, and although I knew that I could do that, so could someone else.

Leighton Ford came to Lansing, Michigan for a crusade, and publicity became my responsibility. As I became acquainted with Dr. Ford and he saw my articles in various magazines, we talked about my future. I remember telling him that I felt pulled in two directions: I enjoyed my student work but had increasing opportunities to write.

Unknown to me, Sherwood Wirt, editor of *Decision* magazine, was looking for an assistant editor, someone with the combination of theological training and journalism. There were many people with one or the other of those qualifications, but few had both. Dr. Ford proposed my name. That began months of correspondence and interviews which eventually brought me to *Decision*. I found that my "wrong turns" had equipped me for what the magazine required! Three years later Sherwood Wirt retired, and Billy Graham asked me to become editor of *Decision*. Whether I stay in this position until I retire or die—or leave before today ends—I now know God has all things in His control. I don't have to see things clearly if I am concentrating on Him. He is more concerned about my life than I could ever be. My first priority must be a willingness to follow Him. He has a claim on me, and I can say, as Paul did, that "all things work together for good to them that love God, to them who are the called according to His purpose" (Rom. 8:28). Each of us can claim that; and in bad times and good times we can live by it every minute of our lives.

Years earlier I had said to God, "All right . . . but whatever happens, it's all Your fault." He could have said to me then what He said to Habakkuk so many centuries before. Maybe He did say it, but I wasn't listening: "I am doing a work in your days that you would not believe if told" (Hab. 1:5, RSV).

None of Us Can Anticipate
God knows what He is doing with us even when we don't. We may cry out for understanding, but most of the time we wouldn't comprehend an explanation because we don't really understand ourselves or our world. None of us can anticipate what is coming in our lives. We can't see down the road. The comforting news is—God can!

God used each apparent "wrong turn" in my life and prepared me for the next step I was to take. He made it all fit together. Will it all "fit together" tomorrow and the day after that? I believe that it will. Since God began a work in my life—as He has in every believer's life—I can't believe that He will stop. He doesn't do things halfway.

Just as I was ready, even expecting, to blame God for the failure that I was certain would come, I can't take credit for any of the good things that have come. It wasn't through my wisdom, it was His careful leading. What has happened is indeed "all His fault," and I am grateful.

We can trust God. He isn't the one we have to worry about. Our main concern must be our commitment to follow Him, making sure that nothing is ever allowed to interfere with our availability or willingness to obey. He alone knows our tomorrows. It is good to see how God works. He has a plan, and in working it out He wastes neither preparation nor experience.

He uses everything that we are, and at each step of the way equips us for the next step ahead. Knowing this provides a wonderful security. It is the only satisfactory way to live. There are no accidents with God. He doesn't take "wrong turns."

We need to know that. Scripture tells us: "If you leave God's paths and go astray, you will hear a Voice behind you say, 'No, this is the way; walk here'" (Isa. 30:21, TLB). "The good man does not escape all troubles—he has them too. But the Lord helps him in each and every one" (Ps. 34:19, TLB).

A Satisfying Life

We all want to have a satisfying life. People who lament that they have made a mess of their lives have not done so because they wanted to. They didn't intend to do it. They started out seeking happiness but took wrong turns, perhaps looking for pleasure and joy as experiences rather than what they really are—the by-products of a fulfilling minute-by-minute, day-by-day walk with God.

A life of satisfaction comes not through the elimination of struggles or hard times or pain. Quite the opposite is true. Often those who have the easiest times think of themselves as enduring the greatest hardships, while others who have gone through great trials have expressed having a basically satisfying, even easy, life.

So much of how we live is based on our perspective. What is your measurement for your life? For what do you look? What do you want in life? Some of us look the wrong way even when we are looking for the right things. God said to Isaiah, "Look unto the rock whence ye are hewn" (Isa. 51:1). Those are not empty words. That is a contact, a reference point for a satisfying life.

We Can Keep On

We know the stories of inventors, statesmen, millionaires who have practiced persistence. They kept on. They took what came, made the best of every situation, and went on. If they stumbled, they got up. If they were sick, they took it as valuable time for reflection, prayer, reorganizing their thoughts and plans—and they kept on.

Though persistence can be a stubborn inability to read the signals, it can also be a singleness of purpose to which all events and circumstances contribute. God owns believers; God will teach believers through prayer, the Scriptures, Christian counsel, and circumstances. Knowing that, we can persist. We can keep on. More than that, in these days of confusion when people around us don't know what direction to go and as a result go off in many unsound, immoral, profligate, or illegal ways, we won't. With our eyes on the Saviour, we can keep on.

Your priorities will make your life. You will have more to give because you will have purpose and direction. Under God you will have plans for your time; under God your life will have importance. The plans that you make will not be selfish plans, they will be plans determined prayerfully before God.

The Dictates of God

I know a man who says yes to every invitation he receives. Yet there is no way that he can do everything that he is invited to do, especially when there are three different events scheduled at the same time. He accepts them all, even though he cannot do them all. He just doesn't show up for some of them. This reveals not only a terrible ego problem; it is rude and inconsiderate. It is saying, "I don't think enough of you to refuse or to allow you to find someone else." It is saying, "I am more important than anything you or anybody else does." Because he has no priorities, he has no discipline and he regularly hurts others.

We had better not be spiritual in our talk if our behavior fails to honor God. Self-discipline says, "I can say yes and I can say no by the dictates of God: prayerfully, obediently, lovingly, with awareness that others are under the direction of God as well." That makes for a very satisfying life.

By setting priorities we protect ourselves as well as others. Without priorities, our personal ego needs will rule us and may hurt others.

One afternoon my wife, Andrea, and I were invited to a picnic on the south lawn of the White House by then President Jimmy Carter and Mrs. Carter. It was an enjoyable afternoon; there was music and food and visiting and an opportunity to stroll through the White House and the yards. There were opportunities to visit with the Carters as they moved among their guests. Cameras were allowed and for a while Andrea and I watched people with their cameras. They would rush up to President Carter, sit down beside him for 20 or 30 seconds while a friend snapped a photo, and then jump to their feet and leave. I kept thinking, "How inconsiderate! He is not a subject to be photographed. He is a person, an individual of value. He is not here for photographing; he is a person worth treating as a person." Later, as Andrea and I visited with the President, we left our camera behind. We determined to be guests, not photo-hounds. My wife and I talked with the President about his recent trip on a paddle-wheel boat down the Mississippi River. We talked with Mrs. Carter about *Decision* magazine, because she reads it.

We need to be as protective of others as we are of ourselves. No one likes to be used. At Christian gatherings, users are so eager to "meet" the famous people that they rush across the room to do it, deserting those they had been happily talking with a few minutes before. It seems they need to have this contact to somehow build themselves up because of "whom they are with," not realizing that these people don't like to be used. Nor do people like to be left alone when someone more interesting walks into the room. Be protective of others. They are worth as much as you are. Don't use them.

Enjoy Who You Are in Christ

We have all heard about sales trainers who teach salesmen to get to know the secretary because "she will open doors for you." Some of us treat our brothers and sisters in Christ that way too. We are as responsible to help others build satisfying lives as we are to live satisfying lives under God ourselves. We are not to manipulate people. Jesus didn't; neither should His followers. "The thief cometh not, but for to steal, and to kill, and to destroy; I am come that they might have life, and that they might have it more abundantly" (John 10:10). Jesus is our example.

What a blessing it is to enjoy others because you enjoy who you are in Christ. You are pleased with what God is doing with others because you are pleased with what He is doing with you. How good it is to help others develop and grow because you are developing and growing and don't feel threatened. That is satisfaction in Christ, and you can measure the value you put on your life in Christ by the value you put on others.

We in Christ are rich, not because we know "important" people but because we are important people. We are children of God. Knowing that, enjoying that, gives the pleasure of a satisfying life.

There are thousands of promises to believers in the Bible. God gave them for us to depend on. The God-centered priorities of a believer open the door to the privilege of appropriating those promises.

Give your life totally to God. Let Him help you establish your priorities. You will move out of the narrow inlets of a little life into the broad ocean of abundant living. After all, isn't that what Jesus came to give? Isn't that what He wants for you? Put first things first. Live under the priorities of God.